MY JUPITER
"The Book"

BY
D.A.Gladwin

My Jupiter "The Book"
By D.A.Gladwin
PAPERBACK 2016
Printed in the United States of America

© 2006, 2007, 2016 By D.A.Gladwin
Published by Dan Gladwin, Inc./DBA D.A.Gladwin, Inc.

All rights reserved. No part of this publication may be reproduced, stored in a retrieval system, or transmitted in any form or by any means – electronic, mechanical, photocopy, recording, or any other – except for brief quotations in printed reviews, without the prior permission of the publisher.

Book layout, design and all interior sketches by D.A.Gladwin.

All poems (including those on the web site) are copyrighted.

Library of Congress
Copyright Office
101 Independence Avenue, S.E.
Washington, D.C. 20559-6000

MY JUPITER
"The Book"

GROWING UP IN JUPITER
IN THE
FIFTIES AND SIXTIES

BY
D.A.Gladwin

•••
NOTE
"The Book"
was added to the title to differentiate this book
from the original little "Fat Pamphlet."

The "**WHY I WROTE IT!**"
(two pages further)
might explain it better.

•••
"Two Fishers   Front Cover
sketch
on the Loxahatchee River"
(Pen & Ink)
and
Rear Cover
sketch
"Reflections"
(pencil)

By
D.A.Gladwin

•••
NOTICE
this book may not be suitable for all ages.

*I would guess
that it would get
at least a PG–14 rating.*

In memory of
my (younger) brother
"JAKE"
(Stephen D. Gladwin)

WHY I WROTE IT!

Well, the truth is – sometimes 'free time' and 'being bored' can get you in trouble, but sometimes they just lead you down a new path. I was bored and had some free time – and, I definitely didn't need any more trouble, so I started writing. As it happened, I never intended for this story to go any further than the hard–drive of my computer (at least until I was long gone!), or I never would have had the nerve to write something so personal.

{I once had the opportunity to read a letter of a long past relative, and I remember how much I enjoyed knowing a little something about someone from my past. That letter did influence both my decision to write this book in a more personal way and also my decision to add in some of my poems and sketches. So, yes, this book might better have been called THE BOOK OF DAN in lieu of MY JUPITER.}

It was only after printing off a few copies for my family and a few (very close) friends that I realized that what I had written seemed to spark a lot of fond memories for people – memories of their own 'growing up' years. That initial positive feedback gave me the courage to go further. From there, (without any proof reading, spell-checking, or otherwise) I printed up what I had written thus far – the ninety-nine pages that I called the "Fat Pamphlet."

The responses to the 'Fat Pamphlet" were, well, I don't know how to describe them – they were just really neat! People sent me pictures of the fish they had caught; some wrote about similar experiences to mine – both in Jupiter and in other areas where they grew up. For example:

An old classmate wrote that no one ever believed her when she described wading up to her knees in mud – just to go swimming. Or, that she actually went rattlesnake hunting ON DATES!

A lady wrote about coming to Jupiter years ago to visit her grandparents and taking the Jungle Cruise trip all the way from Riviera Beach up the Loxahatchee River to the camp of our local legend 'Trapper Nelson'. In her words – "I remember the sense of wilderness back there with a panther in a cage that seemed as if it would burst out at any moment and gobble me up. Trapper's big, bare chest was a bit fascinating and intimidating also."

One guy who is ninety-three (Yeah! 93) wrote me a three page hand written letter describing how he had come down here for the winter in 1951 and '52. A construction worker; he planed to spend his winters down here working. Right after buying a lot in 1952, the company he worked for got the contract for the New York transit system – needless to say, he never made it back here.

My own wife was reminded of her childhood in coastal North Carolina. She remembered bugging her mother as to when she could finally go barefoot for the rest of the summer. Her mother's stock answer was always the same, "when the Bumble Bees fly." My wife had always thought that was her mothers way of saying, "WHEN I SAY SO, THAT'S WHEN!," but then when her eighty-six year old mother commented that my story about going barefoot reminded her of Brenda (my wife) always wanting to go barefoot. She proceeded to explain that where she grew up, they had always used the sightings of Bumble Bees as a sign that there would be no more cold snaps. It was time to put out summer plantings and such – and, yes, time to put your shoes away for the summer. My wife finally understood "when the Bumble Bees fly."

That kind of response would encourage anyone! It sure encouraged me, and so, I got a competent person *{well ok, lets be honest – it was my brother-in-law}* to help me with my spelling and punctuation, And yes, my grammar and sentence structure – BUT, not to the point of making this an 'English Class' assignment.

I wrote more stories and expanded my "Fat Pamphlet" into this book *{Yes! That is why you see "The Book" on the cover}*. Hopefully it will bring up some good memories for you and maybe a few laughs too. Or, at least make you realize, "You weren't the only one that did stupid things while 'Growing Up'." As for the poems, well as I stated earlier, they're personal, they're 'ME' and they are a lot like the pages of the book – memories – simply written in a simple way by a simple guy who remembers a simpler time.

Thank You's
(and apologies)

*This book is dedicated to my family
without whom,
I wouldn't have any stories.
With special thanks to my lovely wife Brenda for putting up
with me for these thirty-five plus years.
And to my wonderful son Guy for helping me to remember
(and in some ways, re-live) my childhood.*

...

*I wish to <u>publicly</u> thank my OLDER brother Skip
for reading the "Fat Pamphlet" FIVE TIMES
and then wanting more copies to give away—
which started the ball rolling.*

...

*And to apologize to my OLDER sister Gerry
for always giving her such a hard time {Yes, including
spelling her name with a 'y' instead for her preferred 'ie'}
and to my little sister Gail (we call her 'Bugs) for hardly
even mentioning her name.*

...

*I also wish to thank my brother-in law
Dr. Gary (Tuck) Rolison who has
more degrees than a compass –
in subjects like physics, astronomy, and the like –
{Yeah! Nothing in writing or English.}
for using his heart as well as his brain
in helping me with correcting and editing.*

...

*Very importantly, this book has, in large part, 'happened' due
to the kind words and inspiration of Ron Wiggins, columnist
for the Palm Beach Post.
Without his encouragement I would not have gone further.*

FOREWORD

To start with, I have always thought of the folks that came to this area before Flagler's train, in other words sometime before about 1900, as the true 'Pioneers' of Jupiter. Those of us whose families came between 1900 and about 1950 could probably be considered 'Old Timers' at this point. My grandfather started coming to West Palm Beach in the '20's and coming up to Jupiter in the '30's, but most of the kids I played with as a child, like the Pennocks, Seabrooks, Brookers, etc., had Grandparents who came here long before that. So, I always considered them to be 'Pioneer Families' and we were 'Newbies'. Now, at least, I can consider my family as 'Old Timers'.

(And disclaimer)

I'm always jokingly saying to people, "It's your story, tell it anyway you want to." Well, this is my story and, I'll tell it, "anyway I want "too!" I am sure I have some things "not quite right" or, "not quite the way someone else remembers it!" But as I said, "it's my story" and it is told "to the best of my recollections."

POEMS

THE RIVER OF MY YOUTH	*1*
AUGUST SUN	*7*
I LOVE TO WATCH THE HERON	*10*
RIVER OF MEMORIES	*13*
THE BALM OF NIGHT	*17*
ME, MYSELF AND I	*24*
I HAVE SEEN A TREE	*29*
I WAIT	*31*
NOVEMBER MORNING MIST	*35*
"PISSED"	*44*
ODE TO THE OSPREY	*52*
TRAIN WHISTLE, TRAIN WHISTLE	*58*
WISE OLD OWL	*67*
THE EVENING	*71*
I LEFT HER – BACK THERE!	*76*
MORNING'S FOGGY FINGERS	*81*
I SEE YOU!	*86*
EARLY IN THE EVENING	*87*
A SOFT SUMMER RAIN	*90*
TINY WHITE LIGHTS	*94*
WHERE HAVE YOU BEEN?	*100*
ALL THE WORLD	*104*
DAMSELS AND DRAGONS	*108*
HAND SAWS	*115*
I TOOK A WALK	*120*
THE PELICAN	*132*
OLD DOG, YOUNG DOG	*143*
HAVE YOU EVER WONDERED?	*149*
OLD TREE	*158*
MUSIC IN THE RAIN DROPS	*160*
THE RIVER'S GONE	*166*

CHAPTERS

DUBOIS YEARS..14
INLET & PLANTATION FLOOD...............................20
STORM WAVES & INTRACOASTA.........................23
ANCHORAGE OR SOUTHARD'S POINT..................26
PENNOCK POINT – HOUSE....................................30
PENNOCK POINT – DAD...25
PENNOCK POINT –BLOCK WALL...........................30
INLET & PLANTATION FLOOD..................................8
STORM WAVES & INTRACOASTAL.......................11
SKI JUMP...32
GO-CARTS, DRUKA, KITES, & MORE....................36
GATORS, HUNTING, STILLS, & OYSTERS..............45
SNOOK, MY BOAT, MY HOUSE.............................49
PENNOCK'S PLANTATION & DAIRY......................53
TRAINS, MAIL, STEIN'S...59
CHURCHES & PADDLE FANS................................63
OWLS..68
PADDLE WHEELERS & RATTLESNAKES................73
SCHOOL...77
SCHOOLS, MOM, & SMOKING..............................82
CHICKENS...88
TRAPPER'S AND THE JUNGLE CRUISE.................91
MODES OF TRANSPORTATION............................95
LIGHTHOUSE RESTAURANT.................................97
  BEACH ROAD & FRUIT FIGHTS..........................101
  GLYNN MAYO & DRIVE-THRU BARS..................105
  GROWTH OF AREA AND ME...............................109
  GROWTH OF AREA – CHANGES.........................116
  U. S. #1 AND A1A BRIDGES................................121
  CENTENNIAL, DIVE CLUB, CUBA........................127
  THEATERS AND THE HUT...................................129
  NEW YORK, NEW YORK......................................133
  PAL, PRINCE & PAUPER, BLAZE, DAWG............144
  SANDSPURS AND GOATHEADS.........................151
  GOOD AND BAD...159

12

THE RIVER OF MY YOUTH

I SIT AND WATCH MY RIVER,
THE RIVER OF MY YOUTH.
IT SEEMS TO HOLD SOME SECRET....
SOME UNKNOWN HIDDEN TRUTH.

I KNOW IT HOLDS THE MEMORIES OF
A TINY LAD GROWN UP.
MEMORIES OF SO MANY THINGS
WHEN WE LOOK AT LIFE CLOSE UP..

FOR I REMEMBER FIRST FISHES,
I CAUGHT FROM THE DOCK.
REMEMBER FIRST KISSES,
WHEN ARMS INTERLOCK.

I REMEMBER THE BOAT,
I FIRST CALLED ALL MY OWN.
I REMEMBER THE FRIENDS,
I CALLED ON THE PHONE.

THE RIVER WAS OURS,
TO EXPLORE ITS DOMAIN.
AND LORD OF IT ALL,
WE WOULD REMAIN.

THE RIVER ALSO HOLDS THE TRUTH
TO SECRETS I'LL NOT TELL.
SOME OF WHICH,THE MEMORY OF;
I WOULDN'T WANT TO DWELL.

*I hope you will read (or have read)
"Why I wrote it" and the "foreword"
because I think that both of them will help
in your enjoyment of
MY JUPITER.
Thanks Dan*

I
DUBOIS YEARS

My earliest memories start at DuBois Park. Folks by the name of Vickers owned the old 'DuBois' house on the oyster mound; they had bought it from the DuBois's years before. The county bought the house from them and bought the rest of the park from the DuBois's. Anyway, we were living in that house when I started first grade. I always have great memories of DuBois Park, many of them at later times then when I lived there, but a few from that early age.

Several memories stand out, one was going through a hurricane while living there. As a little kid, I was scared. Heck!

I'd probably still be scared as an adult! I think I mostly picked up on the fear of my Mother since I was hardly old enough to know what to be 'scared of,' but I'm not sure. I do remember the noise and I remember the screens on the front porch. The screens were made of copper at that time and were pretty strong. The ones that didn't blow out looked like they were covered in some kind of green slime. The tree leaves had been pulverized into tiny bits as they were literally pushed through the screen. The 'goo' was what was left clinging to the inside of the screen. I have always surmised that, that old house has withstood so many hurricanes so well just because it is on that hill. I think the wind hitting the side of the hill shoots upward breaking the force of the winds directed at the house. It seems to create an almost 'calm' area just a few feet back from the steep rise of the hill. The stronger the wind, the stronger the 'reaction' becomes, at least, that's my theory. But, on to memories!

    I remember being five or six years old, it was Christmas and I had gotten a little 'sit on' steam roller. I'm riding my new steamroller down that oyster shell driveway. Remember, I'm a 'Florida Boy' so, to me that driveway was the steepest hill in the state. The 'Ralph Nader's' of the world hadn't gotten started yet; so, I'm sure, that metal steamroller wasn't the safest thing known to man. I'm rolling down the hill – barefoot I'm sure, since children's shoes weren't even invented for this part of the world – so 'brakes' weren't an option. And, who comes heading up the hill to see my new toy but Zeke Kendt! Now he is probably only two or three at the time and tiny (if you can imagine a 'tiny' Zeke Kendt); I don't have the 'brake' option, so I end up mowing him down. Needless to say, I not only lost my 'driving' privileges, 'they' confiscated my equipment! To this day, I don't have any idea what ever happened to that steamroller, but I know I never saw it again.

I remember another time at DuBois's when I thought I was the captain of my domain. This time it was toy boats. I had gotten a little set of plastic boats. You know the kind, they all came in a little clear plastic bag. Something you'd find at a souvenir store. Probably cost all of forty nine cents at the time, but they were everything to me. I was Captain of my fleet! We were down at the beach, right there in front of the park at the Inlet Beach. I'm building shipping channels in the sand and overseeing my fleet when 'some diversion' came alone. Could have been a ghost crab or a sea gull, you know, at that age – 'a diversion'. Well, the next thing I know, it's getting late, time to go! We head up the beach, and I remember my 'fleet'. When I run back to get them, they're NOT there! I still think my Dad had something to do with that! Even though he may not have even been down there on the beach with us. You know, one of those 'life's lessons' you need to learn at an early age!

I also remember watching my Dad build a boat on the porch. Everyday for what seemed like forever, he would get home from work and go out on the porch to work some more on that boat. Years and years later I can remember going down to the DuBois's docks and seeing that boat that my Dad had built among John's (DuBois) 'fleet' of rentals. The boat he built was only twelve or fourteen feet long with an almost flat bottom like most of the other boats that John owned. This one was just special because my Dad built it and that just made it 'better' than all the others.

John rented boats out to whoever wanted to go out on the river to fish or just to have fun. Most were just row boats with a set of oars; a few had small outboards. When the bluefish (or almost anything else) were running, everyone in town it seemed took one of those boats and headed out the inlet. I can remember Mom as she looked from the porch, waiting for Dad to come back in. Often the boat would be so full of fish that there was barely any freeboard left above the water line. Navigating the inlet with only three or four inches of freeboard wasn't easy but they 'almost' always made it, at least Dad always made it!

The one thing, looking back at the "DuBois House" days, that now seems most memorable is how happy my Mom sounded whenever she talked about living there. You could just tell that she had loved living there. I think she loved that there were always other people around. She just loved 'people', and I think when we moved from there she missed that.

Even when I got older, we would often come back to DuBois's while Mom visited everybody or Dad went fishing. I still remember climbing up those angled coconut trees and cabbage trees and seeing how hard you could get them to bounce – usually to the point of bouncing you right off. One person climbed up and 'saddled' the tree and the others would get the tree bouncing as hard as they could to try and bounce you off. Today's mechanical bulls have nothing on those 'bucking' trees.

AUGUST SUN

WHITE HOT SPARKS
OF AN AUGUST SUN

SCATTERED BY THE WAVELETS
OF A WEST WIND

BURN RED THE FACE
OF THE FISHERMAN

SWEATING IN THE HEAT
OF THAT WEST WIND

SHADED FROM THE RAYS
OF THAT WHITE HOT AUGUST SUN

BY THE GREAT WIDE BRIM
OF A BRIGHT WHITE PANAMA HAT!

DAG

II
INLET & PLANTATION FLOOD

Another thing I remember, or at least, 'think' I remember happening at DuBois's was when the inlet filled over *{one of many times as I understand}*. You know how some childhood memories are actually just memories of 'remembering other people reminisce?' This may be one of those times! But, I do know what they did! They waited until after some very hard rains and the tide was just right and everybody young and old went out there with a shovel or hoe or whatever they had and helped dig a little ditch from the river to the ocean. I say little because it didn't have to be very big, maybe three to five feet deep and wide enough that the sides didn't cave in. With that many people it went pretty fast. Once the water started flowing from the river, it didn't take long to have an inlet again. In fact, within minutes, the people on the north side needed help getting across to the south side where they had all come from. It would have been a long walk back if you were stuck on the north side because there was no Jupiter Inlet Colony, that side of the inlet was just swampy land with a lot of cabbage trees. It was only later that it was filled in with dredging material from either the Inlet or Intracoastal Waterway.

It was probably during that Inlet closing that we had the only 'real flood' that I kinda remember. I was awful little at the time, but I know the water was at least three feet deep over all of Pennock Plantation (now, Jupiter Plantation Development) and all of Center Street and beyond. Dad was rowing a rowboat down Center Street to get to Pennocks to help out. *{Come to think of it, these two things could not have happened at the same time. Somehow I associate my arm being in a cast, well actually wrappings and a sling, while watching the inlet work. Seems my curiosity had gotten the best of me (again!) when I had to investigate a big pot of boiling cooking oil Mom had going on the stove. She was making donuts! Yeah! I still have the scars. I don't remember the pain or anything else about it other than a fear that I was going to lose my arm. But, I'm not sure I picked up that idea from the adults or anything. No, I have a feeling that came from my older brother not wanting me to do something or play with something – you know how "older brothers" are! And, I know I was healthy when I was riding in the back of that rowboat.}*

Everyone was up to their waist in water trying to pick up the flats of ferns that they grew at the Plantation and put them on top of the work benches that lined the slat houses. There were acres of slat houses that created the shade needed to grow the ferns. The work benches were kitchen counter height and that is thirty six inches, and the water was just over those benches – and, that's why I know the water was at least three feet deep! I'll come back to Pennock Plantation sometime. later in my story

I LOVE TO WATCH THE HERON

I LOVE TO WATCH THE HERON STALK
HIS PREY ALONG THE SHORE.
HE HAS THAT SPECIAL 'HIGH-STEP' WALK...
LIKE NOTHING SEEN BEFORE.
...ON STILTED LEGS, BETWEEN THE BLADES
OF TALL SHORE GRASS HE WADES.

NEVER A RIPPLE, NEVER A SPLASH.
THE WATER AROUND HIM SMOOTH AS GLASS.
HE HAS THAT OTHER QUIRKY WAY...
ALL THE WHILE HE STALKS HIS PREY.
HE TURNS HIS HEAD...FIRST LEFT, THEN RIGHT,
KEEPING EVERYTHING IN SIGHT.

BUT WHEN HE TURNS IT STRAIGHT AHEAD,
YOU KNOW HIS PREY WILL SOON BE DEAD.
FOR HIS BEAK IS LIKE AN ARROW
ITS FEATHERS ARE HIS HEAD.
HIS NECK, A BOW, IS PULLED BACK TAUT;
... HE NEVER LETS IT FLY FOR NOUGHT.

SO WHEN HE TURNS TO POINT HIS PREY,
TO LET HIS ARROW FLY.
THERE REALLY IS NO QUESTION THAT,
THAT FISH IS GOING TO DIE.
AND WHEN THE DEADLY DEED IS DONE
HE MAKES IT LOOK LIKE SO MUCH FUN.

WITH A FISH STUCK ON HIS BILL;
WHAT HE DOES, DOES TAKE SOME SKILL!
FOR HE FLIPS IT FLYING IN THE AIR ,
LIKE A FLAPJACK FROM A SKILLET.
AND DOWN IT COMES, ALL TURNED AROUND
AND LANDS RIGHT IN HIS GULLET.

DAG

III
STORM WAVES & INTRACOASTAL

During one storm passing by (this was after we moved from DuBois's), the waves got so big that the 'white water' from the waves (not the actual wave) was washing over the top of the dune and running down to the Intracoastal Waterway. All this was right where the Beach Colony is now. Dad (I think it was Dad) took us across Cato's (previously 'Wood's) bridge. We all had inner-tubes and had a blast riding those 'white water rivulets' from the dune down into the intracoastal. *{ Note: We always called bridges by the name of the bridge tender that worked the bridge. He and his family usually lived in a little house 'hanging' off to one side of the bridge and one shoreline.}* Cato's bridge was a narrow 'side-swing' bridge, two bigger trucks couldn't pass on it and most people not used to it felt that they couldn't either; so they would 'drive down the middle'. When I was older and driving, that used to really 'piss me off', so I would play 'chicken' with them, forcing them to either pull over to the side or back up. That was a cool bridge though! It was a lot of fun to climb up the suspension towers on each side of the draw section and dive off, or to ride the swing-out section while a big tugboat pushed a load of barges through. Imagine being allowed to do that kind of thing today!

There was a lot of commerce on the Intracoastal Waterway at that time. Sometimes six or more barges, loaded with lumber or whatever – being push by one tug. Going south they didn't have much problem, but heading back north on an out going tide they quite often didn't make the corner and ran aground (at the Inlet Colony across from the lighthouse). They could usually get off at the next tide change, but sometimes needed to call in some help. There was a lot more 'big boat' traffic on the Intracoastal then, but a whole lot less 'small boat' traffic. I remember in High School I would see the Presidential Yacht coming and going. That was when President Kennedy came down to his family's home on Palm Beach. We were out skiing once just south of where the Indiantown Road bridge is today and the Kennedy's were out on that yacht. They had a beautiful mahogany ski-boat with them and were skiing the Intracoastal just like us. Gotta say, that Mrs. Kennedy looked pretty good in a bathing suit! But, on to other things and younger times!

One thing we did when we were younger that was a lot of fun, was walk over to the lighthouse with an 'ole piece of cardboard we found somewhere. We'd climb to the top of the steps at the base of the lighthouse, jump on our piece of cardboard and ride it all the way down the side of that sand hill. That was our 'snow'. Tommy Ryan and I used to spend hours doing that!

RIVER OF MEMORIES

I WATCH THE BOATS AS THEY GO BY.
SOME ARE FRIENDS, AND WE SAY,"HI!"
BUT, IT'S THE BOATS WITH A SON AND HIS DAD
THAT SOMEHOW SEEM TO MAKE ME SAD.

I WATCH THE FATHERS...IN THEIR BOATS
PULLING SONS...IN RUBBER FLOATS.
I SEE MYSELF...IN ALL THEIR FUN.
I SEE THE FATHER...IN THE SON.

I SEE MY FATHER IN HIS BOAT,
ME AT THE END OF THAT LONG ROPE.
HE'S YELLING DIRECTIONS...TO LEAN TO AND THRO.
I'M YELLING AND LAUGHING, AND SAYING,"LET'S GO"

I SEE MY SON AND ALL OF OUR FUN.
I'M IN OUR BOAT, HE'S ON THAT ROPE.
I'M YELLING DIRECTIONS,
"HEY, DO THUS AND SO."
HE'S YELLING RIGHT BACK,
"COME ON, DAD; LET'S GO"

AND THEN I WATCH...THE BOATS GO HOME.
THE WATER CALMS...AND I'M ALONE.
I BEGIN REFLECTING ON THAT TIME,
WHEN ALL OF THAT WAS TRULY MINE.

I SEE MY FATHER, SEE THE MAN.
I SEE HIS ASHES...NOW THE SAND.
I SEE MYSELF...BECOME THAT MAN.
I SEE MYSELF...BECOME THE SAND.

I SEE MY SON, A MAN BECOME.
I KNOW THE CYCLE...IS NOT DONE.
DAG

IV
ANCHORAGE OR SOUTHARD'S POINT

From DuBois's we moved out to what is now Anchorage Point, at that time is was called Hooley Point or some times Southard's Point – the people who owned it at that time and that's who we rented from. There was a huge plantation house on the tip of the point with groves of mango trees and some huge banyan trees. As a kid, you could spend all day up in those trees and never have to touch ground. One thing that was even neater was that my sister was extremely allergic to mangos so she never ever bothered us when we were up there. If she even thought about it, we would start throwing mangos at her.

At that time Hooley (Anchorage) Point consisted of a big main plantation house out at the end (where the Southards lived) and then some sheds, old servants quarters, and a caretakers cottage about a quarter mile from the main house – that's where we lived. There were some old broken down windmills on the property that we loved to climb, and there were peacocks and banty hens running loose all over the place. Talk about a noise, you can't believe how loud female (the males have the beautiful plumage) peacocks can be – especially at 5:00 o'clock in the morning. Part of the point almost directly across the road from us (about where Bay Harbour now is) had been donated to the Girl Scouts *[1] and that's where they had their Summer Camp – kinda interesting for a young lad like me!

Riverside Drive was a narrow paved road all the way to County Line Road; it had been paved because of Camp Murphy needing it for military proposes during World War Two. There was no Tequesta Drive, Tequesta was yet to be. Everything that is Tequesta now was just woods at that time. There was a wooden bridge where Tequesta Drive bridge is now and then just shell and dirt roads on the other (west) side. The school bus couldn't cross the bridge to pick us up for school, so we always had to walk up the road and across the bridge to get the bus. There was a family of scrubjays that live right next to the bridge on the west side. We would always try to remember to bring some stale bread or at least some crust with us to the bus stop so that we could stop and feed the jays. Scrubjays were never afraid of people, so they would sit on your head, your hand, or whatever while you fed them. Of course, standing around feeding them meant we were on the wrong side of the bridge whenever the bus came. That didn't just mean running across the bridge, it meant running all the way across the bridge and up to Riverside Drive, because that's where the bus turned around after picking us up. And, missing the bus was NOT something you wanted to explain to my father. Mom was a 'piece of cake' about anything, but my Dad was not someone you wanted to reckon with.

We were living in that house on Southard's (Anchorage) Point when dad bought property on Pennock Point, and we began to build a new house out there. When Dad was looking for property, he figured he could swing no more then $1200 total for whatever he bought. Even at that, it was with the idea that he could get the seller to hold paper for him. Dad found two pieces of property on the river that he could buy for that price. One was about twelve acres running from Center Street to Limestone Creek *[2](now the C-18 canal), that property is now where Rio Vista Drive is located. The other property was two of the new riverfront lots that Shirley Pennock Floyd was breaking her property into on Pennock Point, each lot was a about three quarters acre. Dad bought those because the water was deeper for keeping a boat. From the days of building that first boat on the porch at DuBois Park, I don't think there was ever a time that my Dad didn't have a boat of some kind; and, they kept getting larger and larger as time and money progressed.

THE BALM OF NIGHT

THE BALM OF NIGHT SOOTHS SMOOTH
THE RIVERS WRINKLED FACE OF DAY,
AND THEN THE LIGHTS BEGIN TO PLAY,
LIKE STRANDS OF GOLD AND SILVER LACE
THEY LAY ACROSS HER SILKEN FACE.

AND FROM MY QUIET PLACE
I LOOK UPON HER FACE
AND CONTEMPLATE MY SPACE
A PLACE SO SMALL, A SPACE SO LARGE.
I'M LOST IN IT ALL.

THE BALM OF NIGHT SOOTHS
SMOOTH THE RIVERS WRINKLED FACE OF DAY,
AND THEN THE LIGHTS BEGIN TO PLAY.
THEY LAY ACROSS HER SILKEN FACE...
LIKE STRANDS OF GOLD AND SILVER LACE.

I LOOK UPON HER FACE,
FROM MY QUIET PLACE
AND CONTEMPLATE MY PLACE.
SO SMALL A PLACE, SO LARGE A SPACE .
I'M LOST IN IT ALL.

DAG

V
PENNOCK POINT – HOUSE

Pennock Point was nothing more than an abandoned cow pasture that the (Pennock) Plantation had used to run cows on for years. No roads, no houses, nothing – the center was thick woods with a lot of low lying areas. In fact, there was a substantial amount of sawgrass growing in those low areas and that stuff can cut you up every bit as much as the name implies. All this diversity made for a great area for hunting, and horse riding, and just 'screwing around in' – which we did a lot of.

The waterfront was so thick with jungle-like vegetation that it was impossible to get to the river without chopping your way through with a machete. There was a dirt trail running around the point approximately where the present road is now. Loxahatchee River Road was the only 'real' road in the area; it had several homes scattered along its length. It then 'petered out' about where it ends now and from there continued straight on as a sand trail all the way to Trapper Nelson's place.

We began clearing the Pennock Point land by hand with grub hoes and axes. We would wrap a chain around the palmettos and hook the chain to the back of Dad's old four-wheel drive Jeep pickup (the only kind of vehicle we ever owned for many years), as one person was pulling with the Jeep, the other was chopping at the roots with the ax. Little by little we got that land cleared. I also got to learn how to drive a Jeep at a very early age.

Next, was building a house! Actually, the first thing we built was a concrete block garage so that Dad had a place to store the tools and materials we used to continue on with 'a house'. There was no "Rinker" company delivering ready-mix concrete at that time. All the concrete was mixed by hand; Dad did borrow a gas powered concrete mixer to mix the concrete for the footings and (later) the floor and then the beam, but all the rest was mixed by hand in a regular old hand made mortar box. The box was maybe six or seven feet long with wood sides, angled at the ends, and a sheet of metal nailed to the bottom and up each end. I described all this because that box made a great little boat. Heavy as hell and it always would leak and end up sinking to the bottom, but a great little boat if that's all you had.

Whenever Dad needed more materials for the house, he took the truck up to Hobe Sound Lumber. It was always great to go with him because, one, you didn't have to work if you were riding in a truck! And, two, we almost always stopped at the Hobe Sound Ice Plant to get an ice cream sandwich. The ice plant was neat! It was big; they furnished all the ice for packing anything that needed to be shipped cold (like fish) on the trains and for Jupiter Island and anybody else that needed ice. It smelled of ammonia which is what they used as a coolant, and of course, it was COOL inside – the only place that was! And, the ice cream sandwiches were the coldest, best tasting ice cream sandwiches anywhere.

Dad hired George Southard the son of our 'landlords' to help out whenever there was a 'big pour' (of concrete) like the footings or the floor. George was a big guy; he could carry two 90 pound sacks of cement at a time. I even saw him carry three, one on each shoulder and one under his arm. The rest of the work, we pretty much did ourselves. Keep in mind that neither my brother Skip or I weighed more than two concrete blocks and we each carried two of those blocks at a time to build that entire house. And, we laid a lot of the blocks in that house. That garage ended up becoming a part of the main house real quick so that we could move in. It (the garage) was divided in two, half was Skip's and my room, half was my older sister Gerry's room. The rest of the house consisted of one huge flat roofed space with a kitchen and dining area at one end (next to the converted garage), a bathroom built right in the middle, to divide the spaces, and a living room at the other end. The living room also served as Mom and Dad's bedroom.

The wall between the 'rooms' in the old garage didn't go to the ceiling in order to allow air to flow through, remember, there was no such thing as Air Conditioning then. Anyway, that 'wall' became a bit of a problem for my sister as we all got a little older and she began having 'friends' over for the night or even when they just came over for the day since we always went swimming – and you 'had' to change out of that wet suit sometime! Of course, Gerry was quick to inform her friends to 'be careful' when they first showed up at the house. Dad later built another addition with two bedrooms (one for he and Mom, and one for Gerry) a laundry room and a second bathroom. Of course, it was about that time that brother Steve came along. Then six years after that, my little sister Gail. But by that time Gerry was getting married and moving on.

There were five of us kids. My older brother Skip and sister Gerry and then brother Steve six years younger than me and little sister Gail who started first grade the year I graduated from High School. The thing I remember most about my little brother Steve was watching my Mother spend 'hours and hours and hours' teaching him how to lip read and how to talk. He was profoundly hearing impaired, and yet could speak with amazing clarity – thanks to my Mom. His speaking ability was unheard of for someone with his level of deafness. What Mom taught him was a gift and a curse at the same time. When Steve talked, people didn't realize that he was deaf and they didn't realize that he was reading their lips. When there were several people around, and one turned to speak to another, they didn't realize that Steve could not hear what they were saying to one another. This created a great deal of confusion and embarrassment when he was little – and hadn't learned what was happening. When Steve spoke his diction didn't belay his affliction, so that people had no idea what the 'problem' was. I still start to cry when I remember watching him in a group of other little kids. He would stand and watch one person speaking who was directly across from him and begin reading that person's lips. When others were also talking, Steve didn't realize it and when he started to talk it was often in the middle of someone else's conversation, and often about a subject that had already changed. Everyone would start to laugh at him and I'd want to scream at them!

My littlest sister, Gail, seems to have grown up in a whole different family than my older brother, sister, and I. My parents were older, and more financially secure. And, most of all, my Dad seemed to have 'mellowed out' a little. But she also faced a great many more 'other' issues than the rest of us. Not the least of which was our Mother suffering from severe depression to the point that she took her own life when Gail was only twelve. Mom's death changed our entire family's dynamics. Some good, a lot bad; but it did bring all us kids together. Not many years later, Dad began suffering from the onset of Alzheimer's disease. He also got remarried – to a women who had been married to four men before him. All of that created a horror story that I don't even what to go into. But, the end result was that during the course of his illness there were no less than seven new wills created, the last of which disinherited all of his children.

One of the happiest days of my life was when she married number six shortly after my Dad's passing because then, she was no longer a "Gladwin" and people no longer mistakenly thought she could somehow be MY mother. I think I sometimes scared people when I was so forceful about correcting that little 'faux pas." But, lets get back to better times and fonder memories.

Gazabo I
(The Poets Office)
(Pencil sketch)

ME, MYSELF AND I

ME, **MYSELF**, AND **I**
WHEN WE WERE YOUNG
WE TOOK A WALK...
'**I**' KNEW WHY...
'**ME**' WOULD CRY!
... WE HAD TO TALK.

'**I**' WILL TAKE CARE OF '**YOU**!'
'**WHO**?'... '**ME**?'
YES!, '**YOU**'... WITHOUT '**YOU**'
WE'LL HAVE NO PAIN.
'**I**' WILL GIVE US GROWTH AND GAIN!

WE'LL STUFF '**YOU**'...
'**WHO**?'... '**ME**?'
YES !, ... '**YOU**'
WE'LL 'STUFF' **YOU**,
MAYBE HIDE YOU IN OUR SHOE.

'OH!'... IT MIGHT
FEEL STRAINED AND TIGHT!
'YES, IT MIGHT'... HAMPER OUR STYLE;
BUT IT'LL BE FINE... AFTER A WHILE.

IT WILL BE JUST FINE...
'**I**' TAKE CARE OF '**ME AND MINE**'.
'**I**' KNOW WHAT'S BEST,
'**I**' WILL DO THE REST!

NOW!, '**ME**' THINK'ITH...'**I**' WAS WRONG;
THERE MAY JUST BE ANOTHER SONG.
'**ME**' THINK'ITH '**WE**' SHOULD TAKE A WALK.
'**ME**', MYSELF, AND '**I**' SHOULD TALK.

DAG

VI
PENNOCK POINT – DAD

Most of my 'growing up years' were spent on Pennock Point. So I think at this point in my story, I'll 'drop back' and 'start over' and begin the story from there. Instead of 'starting off about me' I think I'll start off about my Dad. Since he was, and still is, a huge part of who I am. Dad was probably one of the most honest, cordial, gentlemen you could ever meet. I never heard anyone, ever, say a negative thing about him – except, of course, us kids. Every man that ever worked for him said great things about what a great boss he was. Every client he ever worked for had nothing but good to say about him. So, maybe it was just us kids? Maybe we just didn't always appreciate him the way others did! Yeah, right! And, maybe you don't know what it's like to have your Mother gently, and very quietly, wake you up at five o'clock in the morning to say, "Your Father's in a bad mood!" When you heard it, you didn't even take the time to go to the bathroom or get a drink of water. No, you headed for the 'hills'. First looking out the window to see where he was and then heading out the opposite way – either sneaking down along the river bank to a friend's house or heading straight out the front door toward the woods. Many a time I would just get into the woods, find a nice soft place (I knew quite a few), lay down and go back to sleep.

But, usually you weren't that lucky. You already knew you were supposed to do such and such chore as soon as you got up – and, definitely, before you 'headed off' anywhere. So you were 'stuck,' you couldn't sneak off somewhere because that would just make it worse! So you made the best of it, dragging out how long you were in the bathroom, how long you could spend cooking a breakfast when you'd normally never think of actually 'cooking' anything. Even at that, you would watch for him to walk around to the opposite side of wherever your 'such and such' chore was, so that you could sneak out and get started on it before he saw you and had 'something else' for you to do 'before' you even got to doing the 'such and such' chore you'd already been told about the night before. Your best hope was that he would end up going off to work or somewhere so that you could finally relax. But, actually, you didn't relax. You worked like all get-out to 'get done' with your 'such and such' so you could 'be gone' before he got back.

Dad didn't believe anyone should sleep past six o'clock in the morning – for any reason! If you were still in bed at six, Dad decided it was time to water the plants. The 'plants' were the ones right outside your bedroom window. Remember! No Air Conditioning at that time therefore, your windows were always opened. And so, you would be awaken by the "lovely feelin' " of getting 'drenched' by a garden hose.

Yeah, Dad was a taskmaster; years later, we could joke that a 'compliment' from our father was 'the absence of a criticism'. He was tough and even our friends had a 'healthy respect' for him. I'll never forget one time when my sister was having a slumber party at the house. The girls were all maybe fourteen or fifteen years old, so I was maybe ten or eleven. Anyway, it's a quiet still night, the windows are all opened, remember, no Air Conditioning. And, every boy in town finds out about this slumber party and, of course, shows up at the house. They didn't actually 'come to the house,' they came to the yard. They were sneaking and crawling all over the place like a bunch of hound dogs when a bitch is in heat! Dad turns all the lights out. He then slips outside with his trusty old 'break' shotgun. Remember, it is a very quiet still night and all those boys had frozen in their tracks for a moment when the lights went out. The next thing you hear is the sound of that shotgun snapping to a 'ready' position. I don't know if you have ever heard some kind of animals rustling in the woods or not, but if you can imagine the sound of ten or fifteen wild hogs being startled in the middle of a palmetto patch; that's what it sounded like as those boys scattered. I don't think I ever laughed so hard in my life – for once, it wasn't ME!

"Still Waters"
(Pencil sketch)
<u>DAG</u>

I HAVE SEEN A TREE

I HAVE SEEN A TREE,
I HAVE WATCHED IT SWAY.
I HAVE SEEN IT MOVE
IN THAT OH SO GENTLE WAY.

I HAVE SEEN A TREE,
I'VE STOOD AND WATCHED IT GROW.
I'VE SEEN EACH LIMB
GROW UP AND OUT,
EACH LEAF IN PLACE JUST SO.

I HAVE SEARCHED THE FOREST OVER
MANY TREES THERE I HAVE SEEN,
DIFFERENT SIZES, DIFFERENT SHAPES,
AND DIFFERENT SHADES OF GREEN.

I CAME TO LIKE THEM ALL QUITE WELL,
THOUGH OTHERS MORE THAN SOME.
AND DEEP INSIDE OF ME I KNOW
THERE IS A SPECIAL ONE.

SOME ONLY THINK A TREE IS GREAT
IF ITS TRUNK IS PERFECT ROUND.
THEY CHECK IT ALL, EACH LIMB
AND BRANCH, TO SEE IF ALL IS SOUND.

SOME ONLY WANT A TREE THAT'S STRONG
NO WEAKNESSES CAN SHOW,
BUT EVERY TREE WILL HAVE ITS FAULTS
AS ANYONE SHOULD KNOW.

<u>DAG</u>

VII
PENNOCK POINT – BLOCK WALL

My older brother and sister always say that I was the only one of us to 'defy' our father. Actually, I wasn't defying him anymore than them; I was just doing what I thought I had to do. When he said "jump," they always asked "how high?" I always just started jumping! For example, one time Skip (my older brother) and I had spent the entire day mixing mud, carrying block, and laying up a wall for an addition to the house. This was during the summer, hot as hell; all our friends are off water skiing or whatever, and Dad's at work. We 'busted our asses on that wall. Also remember that at that time, neither Skip nor I weighed much more than those blocks we were laying. Anyway, when Dad gets home he takes one look at that wall and says it look like "ocean waves" or some other equally obnoxious remark. He then turns and heads on into the house. I proceed to climb up on the scaffolding and 'kick the entire wall down'. I'm assuming 'the wall is unacceptable and has to come down'. Even at that ripe young age of ten or eleven, I knew enough about masonry work (remember, we built that entire house by hand) to know it would be easier to take that wall down that night than to wait till morning when it would have 'cured out' even more. Skip and Gerry thought I was being 'defiant,' I was just 'jumping'. Interesting though, I never had to lay that wall back up, Dad did it himself. Who knows, he might have even learned something from it!

I WAIT...

I WAIT....AND WATCH THE EVENING WANE...
THE STILLNESS OF THE NIGHT.
I WAIT....AND WATCH THE TIDE COME IN,
OR MAYBE OUT;
IT MATTERS NOT WHAT IT'S ABOUT
FOR I LOOK OUT,
ACROSS THE WATERS — QUIET, STILL,
REFLECTING — PERFECT IMAGES
UPON MY MIND!

I WAIT... **"SOMETHING"**
LIKE A SPEEDING BOAT? — DARK, UNSEEN.
"SOUND"
AND THE ARROWS OF ITS WAKE,
"PIERCING"
REFLECTIONS SHATTERED,
IMAGES JUST TINY BROKEN BITS,
UPON MY MIND!

I WAIT...TIME HEALS!
THE TIDES CONTINUES —
IN OR OUT!
IT MATTERS NOT WHAT THEY'RE ABOUT;
FOR I LOOK OUT,
ACROSS THE WATERS — QUIET, STILL
REFLECTING PERFECT IMAGES
UPON MY MIND!
I WAIT...

DAG

VIII
SKI JUMP

There were fun things too! In Dad's construction business they built a lot of seawalls and docks as well as houses. They always kept their "work barge" (actually just a big wood deck with fifty gallon drums packed under it for flotation and a 'home made' steel derrick and winch mounted on it) moored out in front of the house when they weren't using it. That "barge" was the best swimming platform you could ever ask for! We would spend hours out there with our friends diving off the derrick or hiding underneath it, or just laying on it soaking up the sun. The barrels would often rust out and we would have the 'chore' (a fun one for a change) of taking the old ones out (that part wasn't fun, they were covered in barnacles) and 'rolling' new ones back under the platform.

One time, I think they were building a new "barge" or something. Anyway, the derrick and everything were off the old platform and about half of the barrels had rusted thorough so that about half of the platform was under water. We get the bright idea to rearrange the good and bad barrels so that the platform really is 'half' in the water. We then go get the boat and water skis and proceed to try to use this 'half sunk' barge as a "ski jump." Well you know how 'bright ideas' are! We damn near killed ourselves trying to "jump that jump." We did figure out the problem though, it just wasn't slippery enough.

A little of Dad's grease (actually, all of it!) and several quarts of oil and lots of water, and we had a real live ski jump. Thank God we didn't have an "EPA" back then! Anyway, the idea caught on real quick and pretty soon every kid on the river is out with their boat trying out our "ski jump." In fact, it caught on so well that Johnny Lieb (he worked with my Dad) and his boys and several others built a honest to goodness full size ski jump out in front of their house *{Note also, Mrs. Lieb was a Pennock}*. Mr. Lieb even built a set of hand made 'jump skis' making his own steam box to bend the wood and everything. That was quite a ski jump! And to think you'd be afraid you'd get your pants sued off if you did anything like that today!

Another neat thing about Mr. Lieb, he had a big old black Cadillac Touring Car, probably a nineteen thirties or forties model. There were little 'jumper' seats that folded out of the back of the front seats to hold more people. He used to pick us all up in that car to take us to Sunday School every Sunday morning. We didn't miss Sunday School if we could help it, it was a way to "get out of more 'chores'!" That was really a cool car!

Sun Porch
(Pencil sketch)
<u>DAG</u>

NOVEMBER MORNING MIST

NOVEMBER MORNING MIST,
SOFT GRAYS, RICH WET GREENS.

I SIT REFLECTING...DREAMS;
ON THE RIVER'S MORNING MIRROR,

BROKEN ONLY...
BY THE DOUBLE DIMPLES OF AN IBIS
COTTON WHITE WINGS ROWING;

TIPS TOUCHING...
A REFLECTED SELF.

DAG

IX
GO-CARTS, DRUKA, KITES, & MORE

As I've said, we had a lot of fun times on the Point; several times we built (our version of) go-carts. Ours were made of whatever we could find. Stevie Floyd (his Mom was a Pennock) and his Mom had moved on to the Point by this time. Stevie, my brother and I would build these things and run them all around the Point. Our best one was made from a metal bed frame, a very old five horsepower Briggs & Stratton engine, an old Crosley 'rear end,' and I don't remember what for a 'front end'. It was great, our best idea was to mount a permanent 'toolbox' to it! Much later, Mr. Wilson, who owned Wilson's Palm Gardens another good size nursery right on Loxahatchee River Road across from the south Pennock Point Road, let us 'collect up' boxes and boxes of old Model-A parts. We ended up with a complete running Model-A minus the body. But, we did have front fenders and a firewall, so it was pretty cool!

That reminds me of one of our fun escapades with that Model-A – trying to pull ourselves up in the air with a homemade kite. Yeah, we were always full of good ideas! We had all always made kites as kids – a couple sticks, some string, newspaper and a little flour paste and you had yourself a little kite. Well, maybe its a good time to drop back and explain why we always had a little more to work with than the average kid. First, remember that our Dad was a contractor. Second, remember that he used our yard as a storage yard for a lot of materials and 'extra' or 'good used' stuff. And third, Dad had hauled an entire building off of Jupiter Island to use as a storage/workshop. That 'shed' as we called it was great. It was about twenty plus feet wide (they had split it right down the middle – by hand – to get it home on somebody's big flatbed truck) and maybe thirty plus feet long. They put it back together up on block piers. Off the back side Dad built a full length lean-to roof, at the back end of which we created a horse stall and feed/tack area. The rest of that (lean-to) area was used to store the mower and stuff and/or to clear out for working on our cars. The entire inside of this shed was one big workshop with (as things moved along) more and more different types of tool, etc. for us to get in trouble with.

Well, what with the availability of big rolls of plastic sheeting (used to cover lumber, etc.), the opportunity just "presented itself." I probably don't have to tell the whole story here, I think you can get the picture. Suffice to say, nobody got killed! And no, we never got in the air either.

Earlier, I mentioned the horse stall that was a part of shed. We had about an acre of land fenced in as a pasture for a horse we had. She was a little Quarter Horse named Druka, probably a good ten or fifteen years old when we got her. She was quite a horse though, you could shoot a shotgun off her back and she barely flinched. She was a very smart horse. *{Yeah I know, Gerry [that's my sister], it was YOUR horse. I* *know, Dad told you, she was YOUR horse. Yadda, yadda, yadda... you rode that horse what, twice, three times, in your life! I rode her almost every day. I used to hunt off her and ride to Trapper's, often with Sandi Lieb. Heck, you were off to Palm Beach High, or off with your girlfriends chasing boys or off whatever and rarely even saw that horse for Pete's sake. But, I know! It was your horse. Yadda, yadda, yadda...}* Couldn't guess from that little statement that my sister and I ever disagree about anything could you? Yeah! She's just like my older brother – they're both wrong about a lot.

But, back to Druka, she was a lot of fun but she had her quirks also. She refused to cross wooden bridges and we had a lot of wooden bridges at the time – Jones Creek, Sims Creek, Limestone Creek, Steels Creek and more. She did not like looking through the boards and seeing the water *{you probably didn't even know that did you, Gerry!}* so I had to stop at every bridge, get off her, take my shirt and wrap it over her eyes, and then walk her across the bridge.

Another of Druka's quirks was that she loved to get out of her pasture – just for the sake of "doing it!" She could come up with more ingenious ways of breaking down a gate or pulling out the bolts that held the rails in (because she'd already figured out how to get her head between those rails and lift straight up, to take them out of their slots. Once, after we had finally drilled holes completely thru the gate-rails AND the gatepost, and then put a bolt and nut thru everything, we thought she had given up – but it was not to be. Previously, she had learned to first bang against the rails with her nose to loosen the bolt, then stick her head thru the gate rails, turn her head sideways and lift the rail slightly while working the bolt end with her lips until she could finally get the bolt with her teeth and pull it out. Yeah, try imagining all that in you head! As I said, she was a very smart horse.

Anyway, one day, after getting a sore head and bloody lip from trying to get that bolt out all day, she acted as though she had FINALLY given up. I had been watching her earlier, working this gate rail to death when this happened. She walked off, got a long long, drink of water (I think she was trying to get some weight in her girth) and then came back to the rail. She walked right up next to the rail and just leaned over, that simple; the rail began to bend and she just leaned some more – until, all hell broke loose, literally. She did a complete roll-over, hard onto her side, then her back with her feet straight up in the air, then landing on her opposite side. All while boards and bolts and splinters are flying everywhere, and the noise of it all was quite unbelievable too! She lay there for some time. Watching from inside the house, I though for a moment she'd killed herself, having run a big split of railing through herself. But, before I could even get out the door, she stood up, shook herself off and started walking toward the good green grass of the front yard. Druka was a lot of fun. I think she loved the woods as much as I did and we spent a whole lot of time together, that horse and I. Bandit, my dog (I'll tell you about him sometime later) loved to come with us too. *{Little side note. Druka and I had a little 'falling out' toward the end* *there. Not her fault though. It was my worst scare up to date and it did land me in the hospital for a pretty good amount of time. I fully recovered though, just couldn't play contact sports in school which kinda got me.}*

Okay, back to another one of the 'not so bright' things we used to do while living on the Point, in fact, maybe more than one! Since I think sometimes they (yeah the "not so bright" things) out numbered the bright things we did. Let's see, first, we all loved to build rockets, and rockets and rocket fuel were not something you just went to the hobby store and bought. Shoot, the nearest store you could have even bought a little plastic model of a rocket would have been Woolworth's Five & Dime in downtown West Palm Beach.

No, we had to improvise. Gun powder and match heads were our 'fuels of choice' and, I'm afraid, necessity. We would collect up every book of matches we could beg, borrow, or steal; just to cut the heads off for rocket fuel. Sometimes we had enough safety matches (book matches) to make a fairly safe fuel, other times we were cutting and scrapping the heads off big wooden kitchen matches – not so safe, since they could light off just with the friction between them. But, truth be told, our most popular fuel was good 'ol gunpowder and as it happened, we ended up with plenty of that. Seems a guy that worked with my dad *{Old guy, drove a jeep pickup and hauled stuff to and from the jobs. But, I think he had a lot more money than my Dad or Dad's partner – In fact, I think he may have even helped them financially at times.}* belonged to a fancy hunting club or something and ended up with boxes and boxes of old shotgun shells. Everything from buck shot to bird shot. These were old shells that only fired maybe fifty percent of the time so they were useless for hunting. But, great for just having fun with – you know "having fun;" like blowing holes thru old refrigerators or abandoned cars.

And, of course, they were great for cutting apart to use as rocket fuel. These rockets were made with most anything we could find from the little copper air chamber caps used in residential plumbing (to keep the pipes from knocking) to big metal tubes we might find and smash one end closed with a sledge hammer. We would clamp or wire little fins and guides onto them, fill them with one of our wonderful fuels, and "send them off." We did pretty good with these thing, nobody got killed or lost any fingers. Stevie *{I'll introduce Stevie again later.}* lost his eyebrows, but that doesn't count! Not that some rockets didn't create spectacular pre-launch explosions; we were just getting a little wiser as we moved along – yes, first hand experience IS a great teacher. We (Yes! I think, all on our own – but probably not!) had come up with using our train transformer and a very long wire to set these things off. Wow! What a life saver – yeah, literally.

Okay! Just one more "stupid boy tricks" and I am off this subject. BB guns, or more specific, the Daisy Red Rider BB gun, I think the only BB gun made at the time. Most every kid (remember, "Kid" in this story almost always means "boy") had a Daisy from about the same time they had pocket knives (That was early, but I'll get to them later). BB guns – we all had them, we all were fairly good shots with them, AND, WE ALL KNEW THE RULES. We had been taught gun safety from a very early age. But, by the time this happened we were older, we had real guns, and we were very very safe with them. BB guns were toys, shoot you could hit someone in the butt with a BB and they hardly turned around – especially with guns as old and worn out as ours. So sure enough, we end up having a BB gun war – and we had the perfect place.

On the East end of the point, on a long section of shoreline there had been some absolutely hugh Australian Pines with trunks easily two feet in diameter. During some storm, they all got undermined and toppled due east straight out into the water. They made the greatest playground ever, like hundreds of individual wharfs, each with its own "railing post" branches sticking up to hang on to. And, each with more branches and things hanging down for barnacles to grow on and fish to hide in.

Even better was the root end up on shore, because the root system of an overturned Australian Pine looks like a solid wall from the bottom. You can tell that the roots don't even try to ever go down and look for water. They all just mass up within the first six inches of the surface. So there is never anything holding the tree up – the first little wind or erosion and "over they go'. If trees had IQs, then Australian Pines would have to get listed as pretty stupid! But then I'm get'en ready to tell you about us having BB gun wars, so maybe I shouldn't talk. Again, I think I can shorten this up. Yes, I'm the one that got shot in the eye. Yes, I did go blind – at the time! Yes, I did get put in the hospital – again! Yes, my eye did get better! I do have to tell you about the doctor and hospital though. I think Doc. Grogan was around at this point, so we had a Doctor we could get to. But, they were trying to find an eye specialist to get me to, and there were none to be found – anywhere. Seems there was some kind of 'eye doctor convention' in Miami at the time and every single eye doctor was down there. (Geez! Looking back, I don't know how our Mom made it raising us boys. Yeah, I guess, Dad too!) Well, anyway, one of these doctors is heading back this way to pick up some paper he'd forgotten. We hook up with him in the old Como building downtown, he probes, and prods, and pokes at my eye for a while when suddenly I feel a little something fall right into my hands – which were being held 'very nervously' in my lap. Needless to say the whole ordeal was scaring the bejeezus out of me.

He proceeds to tell Mom that I need to stay very still in the hospital for a few days to give my eye a chance to heal. The next day my brother and Stevie come down with my Mom to visit. She heads for the cafeteria for some coffee and we boys head for the halls for some wheelchair racing. The next day, we get stopped from racing, so we take the wheelchairs and start having "wheelie" balancing contest. Looking back, it is a good thing I was good at balancing or I might be blind in one eye today.

"PISSED"

ME, MY DOG, AND I
WENT WALKING, BY AND BY.
I WAS "TICKED." HE HAD SOME TOO,
BUT I TOOK AND SMASHED THEM WITH MY SHOE.

ME, MY DOG, AND I
WENT WALKING, BY AND BY.
I WAS "PISSED," MY DOG HAD TO TOO...
BUT FIRST HE HAD TO "POO-POO."

I WAS STILL "PISSED," SO I SAT ON A STUMP
WHILE HE TOOK A "DUMP," "BOY," IT SURE STUNK!
THEN HE LIFTED HIS KNEE AND STARTED TO PEE.
HE THOUGHT ME A TREE, 'CAUSE HE PISSED ON MY KNEE...
AND IT RAN ALL DOWN IN MY SHOE.
I WAS "PISSED" THROUGH AND THROUGH.

I JUMPED OFF THAT STUMP TO KICK HIS RUMP
AND FELL ON MY FACE IN THAT SLIMY "DISGRACE"
WHERE THE DOG TOOK A "DUMP"
BY THE STUMP..."BOY" IT STUNK!

SO... HEED MY SONG, IT'S DEFINITELY NOT WRONG.
OR ALL TOO SOON YOU'LL BE SINGING MY TUNE.
YOU MAY GET "PISSED-OFF," OFF AND ON;
AND, YOU MAY GET "PISSED ON," ON AND OFF.

BUT, DON'T GET "PISSED ON"
JUST 'CAUSE YOUR "PISSED-OFF!"
AND,...DON'T GET "PISSED-OFF"
JUST 'CAUSE YOUR "PISSED ON!"

DAG

X
GATORS, HUNTING, STILLS, & OYSTERS

I remember sometimes during the rainy season, the river would get so fresh that the larger alligators would start coming down by the house. At night they would lay on the shore with their mouths wide open and their heads just up on the sand, and croak out a sound that attracted the dogs to investigate. As soon as the dog got close enough (often putting their heads right in the gators mouth), the gator would snap his mouth shut and flip the dog right out into the water all in one motion. We almost lost one of our dogs that way, other people were not so lucky. Whenever we saw one of the bigger alligators in our part of the river, Dad (or someone else) would bring out their rifle (Dad used a 30-40) and 'take them out'. It happened quite a bit!

Hunting and shooting were the norm then. Even when we lived at DuBois park, Dad and others would often hunt raccoons which were always a problem. Across the river from the (Pennock) Point where Tequesta Country Club is now, was all woods. A great place to hunt and camp. I spent many an hour just 'plinking' with my 22 right there on the Point. Or, riding our horse out to Trapper Nelson's. There were some great duck ponds *[3] in the area between (what is now) the

Shores, Roebuck Road, Loxahatchee River Road, and what was then called "Steel's Creek *[4]* next to (what is now) Eagle's Nest Development. The dump for the entire North County area was out Roebuck Road, just a shell rock road at the time; it was always a fun pastime to sit out there and shoot rats. Mostly though, I just liked going in the woods, the 'hunting' part was just what I called it!

One thing you did have to watch out for when you were in the woods (besides rattlesnakes) were "Stills." There were a lot of 'moonshine' operations out in the woods at that time. *{ Note: the taxes on "legal liquor" after the end of prohibition made "illegal liquor" very profitable.}* Two or three were right off Loxahatchee River Road north of Pennock Point. The 'moonshiners' did not like you stumbling across their operations. We were scared stiff that we would be shot if one of those guys ever saw us near one of their 'Stills'. We never told anyone but our parents when we did stumbled across one, and they just told us to "STAY AWAY" from it. When we came across one, and, as I said, there were quite a few, we ran like hell in the opposite direction; and once you knew where a particular 'Still' was located, you just stayed away from that area. I have an old smashed up copper 'Still' that I found in the woods near my present home on Riverside Drive. It is smashed up because that is what the 'revenuers' did to a place when they found it!

Another fun (and safe!) thing I remember about Pennock Point were the cookouts my parents and the Brooker family used to have at our houses. Sometimes our house, sometimes their house – actually most everybody in town chipped in – they were just held at our places. *{Note: David Brooker had a charter boat business along with his painting business, and he bought one of the lots down from us [on Pennock Point] and built a boathouse for his charter boat. Not too long after that My Dad's firm (Gladwin – Bassett, Inc.) built them a home there.}* More than fish fries *{which there were a lot of, and most often held to raise moneys for the Volunteer Fire Department or the American Legion Hall – which it seemed everyone in town was a member}*, these were like huge "Clam Bakes," only we had oysters instead of clams. Almost everyone who lived on the water then had some kind of "racks" for cleaning oysters. Weeks before one of these parties, we would all head down to the oyster beds by the railroad bridge and load huge wash tubs – or, for a party, the whole boat – with oysters. When we got back home, we set out all these oysters on the racks we built out under our docks (often old refrigerator shelves or something similar set up on cement blocks). This was done to allow the oysters time to cleanse themselves of sand and grit.

These parties lasted all day and well into the night. There was everything to eat from the steamed oysters; to fried, smoked, and/or broiled fish; frogs legs, usually some venison and/or hog and bowls and bowls of fresh swamp cabbage; and probably lots of whatever fruits, etc. were in season – I just never paid any attention to the fruit. I loved steamed oysters. They were steamed by laying a big piece of tin across your

BBQ pit (after you had a good bed of hot coals), on top of the tin you laid out a mess of oysters (yes! Still in their shell) and on top of them, you laid several layers of wet crokersack *{burlap bags – they were used to cart, carry, and ship everything from frogs, mullet, and snakes, to seeds, stone, vegetables, and fruit }* – pouring more water over them as necessary to keep em' steaming. It only took a moment or two for the oysters to open up, steamed and ready to scoop out, dip in a little homemade sauce and drop in your mouth. Boy, they were good!

XI
SNOOK, MY BOAT, MY HOUSE

I had a small flat bottom boat, not more than ten or so feet long and about three feet wide. I went everywhere in that boat. I rarely used oars, I liked to 'pole'. Just like the "Flats Boats" you see today with the guide standing up on a platform with a long fiberglass pole, I had a nice piece of bamboo and stood on the rear seat and poled everywhere; when the water was too deep to pole, I just used my pole like an oar and paddled across the river. One of my favorite places to go was up Limestone Creek. Before it was dredged into the C-18 canal; it was one of the most beautiful little creeks around. Beautiful clear water with a sandy bottom that was easy to 'pole' and full of fish. I loved going up that creek and "getting away from it all!" You can still see tiny little pieces of that creek, some of the 'bows' that swung out to the north and south are still visible if you know where to look.

Thinking about Limestone Creek reminds me of the time we stopped at Albert Wootens house *[5] on our way out to the Point. *{Albert worked with my dad for many, many years at Gladwin - Bassett, Inc. and his sons and daughter were the same ages as us kids. They later moved to a place on Radio Road.}* When you turned off Center Street onto Loxahatchee River Road; Albert's house was right there on the left (there's a development there now – can't think of the name of it!). Limestone creek ran right by the back of his house.

Their place was just a tiny house with tarpaper covered walls and roof. But, then a lot of our houses weren't much more than that – our house on the point, at that time, was just bare block walls inside and out, and a flat roof. Back to my story, we had stopped by there with my father – I think we had given him a ride home from work or something. Well, when he gets out of the truck, he stops an ask my Dad if he'd like some snook and Dad says "Sure!" Albert then heads into his house, my brother and I are thinking he's gone in to get the fish, but he comes back out and the only thing he's got is his shotgun. He doesn't say a word, he just walks around the side of the house, turns the gun down and "BAM, BAM," he fires off two rapid shots down into the creek. He proceeds to walk down the creek bank and comes back up with two good size snook. TRUE STORY – now that's the way to catch fish!

I still remember the best Christmas present (at least, as a kid, the best present) I ever received was an old used two horsepower outboard motor. Now I had "real power," I could travel to the ends of the earth, or, at least "felt like I could." That motor took me everywhere from Trapper Nelson's (a hell of a long trip) down to Dubois Park. I must tell you an interesting side note also. As a kid, I often took the boat up the North Fork of the river past our old place on Southard's (Anchorage) Point and under the (now Tequesta Drive) bridge. There weren't a lot of houses up there just two or three. But as a youngster one place always caught my eye. It was Harry Jackson's place. He was the secretary for Pennock Plantation for many, many years and it was his brother Doctor Jackson who homesteaded the property *[6]. Anyway, Harry Jackson had built a brand new house in 1925 (probably with the proceeds of selling land in the "Land Boom" of the twenties). It was a beautiful house with a full tile bathroom(a rarity at the time), oak hardwood floors, and cypress ceilings. It was a Mizner inspired style with a two story section that, from the river, looked like a tower, and it had barrel tile on the roof. As a kid, I just always thought that was the neatest house around. That's the house I now live in and have lived in for over thirty years. But, back to my story!

ODE TO THE OSPREY

LIKE THE OSPREY – STANDING TALL
PERCHED SO HIGH, SURVEYING ALL.
HE STUDIES WELL THE TASK AT HAND
FROM HIGH UP ON HIS TREETOP STAND.

WINDS AND TIDES – AND CURRENTS TOO!
THERE'LL BE NO PLAY TILL HE IS THROUGH.
AND, WHEN HE MAKES THE MOVE HE MUST
OFTEN AT THE LIGHT OF DUSK.

THERE IS NO GREAT COMMOTION.
IT'S MORE LIKE..."POETRY IN MOTION."
FROM QUIET CONTEMPLATION
OF A SINGLE MINDED GOAL –
HE MAKES IT LOOK LIKE PLUCKING –
A GOLDFISH FROM A BOWL.

<u>DAG</u>

XII
PENNOCK'S PLANTATION & DAIRY

We spent a lot of time over at the (Pennock's) Plantation (the area is now "Jupiter Plantation," a development) as kids just because it was so much fun playing in the coolness of the fern sheds or building forts out of all the stacks and stacks of newspaper they kept in one of the barns. They used the wet newspaper to wrap and ship the fern in. It was called Plumosa Fern and used in making floral decorations and corsages – apparently, a very popular thing at the time. In fact, a very large area of land including Pennock Point was at one time called Plumosa City, they were trying to separate themselves from Jupiter's taxes (see, some things never change) – but, it never got off the ground.

From the Pennock's Plantation, another great thing to do was to head over to Pennock's Dairy *[7]*. The dairy was about a half mile west of Indiantown Road out where Jerry Thomas Elementary School is now. You can still see some of the huge oak trees that lined the dairy's entrance right next to the Walgreens Store. We would head there because they would always give you a cold bottle of chocolate milk (well, not "always," you had to behave and couldn't abuse the privilege –

like trying to show up every day). Boy, was that good chocolate milk! It rivaled the ice cream sandwich we got at the Hope Sound Ice Plant! Everything, and I do mean, 'everything' from the Plantation to the dairy was pasture land surrounded by woods. Pennock Lane was the original road from the Pennock's plantation to their dairy, but Pennock Lane stopped at Indiantown Road. *{Note: The Only other East-West road was Loxahatchee Drive in front of the school *[8].}* We never wanted to take the road to the dairy because that was the 'long way'. We wanted to made a 'Beeline', but that meant cutting through the pastures where Eastview Manor and Southview developments now are, and those were the pastures where they kept the bulls. Many a time, I found myself running like all get-out to a tree-line in the middle of that pasture to get away from one of those bulls. And, then we'd be stuck there, trying to make it from tree to tree to work our way to the other side; but, you know, it kept life interesting!

Talking about the Chocolate milk reminded me of milk in general at that time. First, it tasted like milk – not this whitish colored water we now call milk. It was thick and it was creamy. It fact, in was delivered right to your door by Ted Ledford (I'll bring him up again later). Milk came in tall quart glass bottles with a fat area in the bottle neck – this is where the cream collected. Of course, it was ice cold, packed in lots of that ice from Hobe Sound and it went right into the refrigerator (Yes! We had refrigerators by that time – NOT Ice Boxes).

So, we ended up having a lot of things made with cream, from real wiped cream to all kinds of cakes and such that used cream. Truth is though, there is really nothing better than ice cold cream poured over your Rice Crispies in the morning. But then "cold cream over Rice Crispies" reminds me of what is even better, "cold cream over cold huckleberries – and, whether there are any Rice Crispies in the bowl is really unimportant at that point.

Early on, when we were pretty much the only family on the Point, we had the huckleberries all to ourselves. Later, when other families move in, and the huckleberries came into season, there was almost a "secret society" amongst families (or at least the kids) to keep from letting on that the huckleberries were ripe. An even bigger secret was where the bushes that you had found were even at, because you wanted to be sure your family got there first with their pans, pails, and buckets before any other family even knew about them. Of course, that rarely worked because it seemed at least one other kid was with you when you found them and then the two of you would just start pickin' and eatin' berries as fast as you could. Somehow, between eating them all in the woods and/or every other creature in the woods usually beating you to the poke anyway, it was rare that you actually gathered enough berries and got them home to your Mom so that she could make a pie. But you often had a couple handfuls that you could hide in the refrigerator and then throw on you Rice Crispies the next morning, or, as I said earlier, just put them in a bowl and pour cold cream over them. And then, to make them taste even better, go stand and eat them in front of your brother and sister – who either hadn't saved any or hadn't been with you when you found them. Yup! That really can add sweetness to the moment!

View from my Gazabo
(Pencil sketch)
<u>DAG</u>

TRAIN WHISTLE, TRAIN WHISTLE

TRAIN WHISTLE, TRAIN WHISTLE,
CLICK-IT-T-CLACK.
TRAIN WHISTLE, TRAIN WHISTLE,
TAKE ME BACK.

BACK TO A TIME,
WHEN TWO COKES WERE A DIME.
BACK TO WHEN TRAINS,
WERE ALL SMOKE AND STEAM.
BACK TO THE YOUTH,
I HAVE IN MY DREAM.

TRAIN WHISTLE, TRAIN WHISTLE,
CLICK-IT-T-CLACK.
TRAIN WHISTLE, TRAIN WHISTLE,
TAKE ME BACK.

BACK TO WATCH MAILBAGS,
SNATCHED FROM A HOOK;
THAT YOU COULDN'T SEE HAPPEN
NO MATER HOW HARD YOU'D LOOK!

BACK TO WHEN WAITING
AT CROSSINGS WAS FUN;
COUNTING THE CARS,
THE ENGINE WAS ONE!

TRY AS YOU MIGHT,
YOU'D ALWAYS MISS SOME....
UNTIL THE CABOOSE,
AND THEN YOU WERE DONE.

TRAIN WHISTLE, TRAIN WHISTLE,
CLICK-IT-T-CLACK.
TRAIN WHISTLE, TRAIN WHISTLE,
TAKE ME BACK.
CLICK-IT-T-CLACK, CLICK-IT-T-CLACK.

XIII
TRAINS, MAIL, STEIN'S

When I was young, a lot of things revolved around the coming and going of the trains. Not so much for me, but for the adults. The Pennock Plantation still shipped their ferns out from the local station which was located where "Johnson Park" is now. Also, a lot of fish and produce, especially oranges were shipped out. There was an orange packing plant on Indiantown Road just west of where the Loxahatchee River runs under the road. It was called Mencer's Groves. We spent a lot of time playing out there during the packing season because Mom would often help them out – washing, sorting, and packing fruit. We also helped, but I'm not sure how much 'real' help we were. I just enjoyed watching it all happen. Everybody used old Model-A's for work trucks back then. Pennock Plantation must have had a dozen or more. Mencer's Groves used them too. Just like the one's at Pennock's, the back of the trucks were just big flat 'decks' made of wood. At Mencer's, they brought the fruit in on crates piled high on those Model-A's. From there they dumped them into huge water troughs for cleaning. At the other end of the troughs a conveyor belt with paddles scooped them up and sent them along a flat conveyor belt where you stood and sorted them for size, color, blemishes, etc. They move through more belts and troughs and

I don't even remember what all until they were repacked for shipping. They loaded them back on those Model-A's and headed for the train station. By the way, most of the trains at that time, at least down here, were good old fashion Steam Locomotives that still burned coal. The diesels and diesel electrics didn't come till later. There is nothing to compare to the sight and sound of a Steam Locomotive, and of course, to seeing that 'Red Caboose' on the end!

The train station was a neat building; I wish they could have kept it. It was moved to a lot near Seabrook Road and converted into a house. By the time I was growing up Jupiter's station no longer handled passengers, you had to go to West Palm Beach for that. It did handle freight, and most of all, it handled all the mail. But, the Mail Train didn't stop. The 'incoming' mail bags were hung on a special 'swiveling' hook on the train and the 'outgoing' bag on another hook on a pole next to the tracks. It was always with great amazement that I watched first, the 'outgoing' mail bag magically disappear from its hook, and almost immediately another 'incoming' bag appeared on the next hook. You would watch it, but it happened so fast that you couldn't really 'see it happen'. One day one of those bags got hung-up and it tore open. The rush of air from the train 'sucked' those pieces of mail all the way to the river. Mail was everywhere and, it seemed, everyone in town was helping to pick up mail. 'Everybody" was probably already there when it happened because the Post Office was right across the tracks, about where the Sub-Shop is now. Everyone came to the Post Office at the same time to get their mail. That was the social gathering place, where everyone caught up on the latest 'happenings' and latest 'gossip' in town.

Right next to the Post Office on the corner of Center Street and Old Dixie was Stein's Sundries. It was a true old fashion 'Drug Store' with the 'soda fountain counter' and everything. Okay, is wasn't a "Drug" store like today. They didn't sell 'drugs' – your doctor gave you any 'drug' that he wanted you to take. It was a 'sundries' store. Anyway, back to my story. Most of us kids never had enough money to buy a 'fountain soda' but every once in a while Mom would spring for one, or we would have worked and saved enough for one. It was a great place. During the summer, a guy would come by every week or two and set up a movie projector in the trunk of his car. He'd run a long extension cord from Stein's and show movies projected onto the side of the building. Every kid, and most of the adults too, sat down there on the grass and watched a movie – remember, there was no TV at that time either – so that was a huge treat.

To give you a little idea of just how small and quiet it was back then, consider this! When you stood on the dock at our house on Pennock Point, which faced northeast, and looked around, the <u>only</u> lights you could see were the red lantern on the railroad bridge and the lighthouse. Really, it was that dark! There were a few houses on Riverside Drive (my Grandparents lived there), but they were mostly fishing cottages that people stayed in for short periods of time during the season. Or, they were like my Grandparents house and tucked back in where you didn't notice them. The Center Street side of the river was developed, and was full of large older homes from the railroad tracks to well past the Plantation. *{In fact, several of those home which are still there today are the famous "Sears homes" ordered directly from the Sear Robuck and Company catalog sometime in the late thirties or early forties. They came complete with everything from the kitchen sink to the roofing material pre-packaged and ready for installation. From what I've heard, it was a real "happening" when the train showed up with several cars loaded down with "your house." And, I would imagine it took quite an effort to off-load all the materials for an entire house considering that you couldn't just run out and rent a crane or forklift or even a truck big enough to carry some of those bundles of materials.}*

XIV
CHURCHES & PADDLE FANS

Actually, next to school, church was the primary 'social scene' for us as kids. It seems we went back and forth between the People's Congregational Church (now the Beacon Baptist Church) on Center Street *[9] and the Southern Methodist Church (now the Jupiter Presbyterian and Reformed) off Center Street on the corner of Town Hall Avenue and Park Street *[10]. I think we mostly went to one church or the other based on what kinds of "kids' programs" they had at any one time, not the quality or the message of the sermons. I remember there was a big 'stink' when the Congregational Church began showing movies in the Rec-hall. Oh! That was a sin in the eyes of the Methodist, or at least some of them. One of the really fun things to do over at the Methodist Church had nothing to do with the church it self. The old original Jupiter Town Hall used to be there. It had been a big (for its time) building. *{As a side note, all of those blocks – hand cast in a 'single making' block machine – were hauled up to US Hwy. #1 to build the American Legion Building. We <u>all</u>, kids and parents alike loaded and hauled, and unloaded, those blocks in our father's pickup trucks and then re-laid them. It is also worth noting that when it was finished, the Legion Hall was one of the biggest building around. Now it*

seems tiny and lost across the highway from St. Judes Church.}
The American Legion and their parties and Forth of July Celebrations are a whole other story, but they'll have to wait for another book. Back to my "church" story. That Town Hall building had also held the Police Department <u>and</u> its jail. All that was left of that building after they tore it down were two huge iron cages. The 'jail cells;' their doors were locked closed and big 'escape' holes had been cut into their sides. The fun part was convincing some 'new kid' to climb inside. As soon as they did, everyone of us, and, it did take all of us, would roll the 'cage' over. There was no way that kid was ever going to get out of that cage by himself. More than once, too many kids headed in to Sunday School early and then there weren't enough of us left to get the cage rolled back over. Then, we were stuck letting on to the adults what we had done!

While I'm on the subject of churches. It seems like a good time to talk about fans. *{Boy I love this writing thing! At work, you always have to stay on task. With this, "It's your story, tell it anyway you want to" attitude – you just head off on any 'ol tangent.}* When we think about paddle fans today, we immediately think, "Ceiling Fan." But back at the time I am writing about, a paddle fan was something you found in the hymnal rack on the back of each pew. It was a piece of cardboard six or eight inches square stapled to a little stick (like a long popsicle stick). Depending on what church you were in, it might have a picture of Jesus on one side and some scripture message on the other side. With everyone all 'decked out" on a hot Sunday morning, you would see hundreds of these little 'paddle fans' waving back and forth all during the service.

In truth, no one had ceiling fans at the time, they were just too expensive. About the only ceiling fans you saw anywhere were the ones downtown at Sears, Robuck and Company or Montgomery Wards – and, you could always notice where they were without looking up because there was always a large oil stain on the floor right under them. All the original old ceiling fans had a little oil reservoir that needed to be filled about once a year. Between spilling a little oil whenever you tried to fill that little reservoir and the fact that if you put too much oil in, the fan would drip, over the years, that spot on the floor got bigger and bigger.

Most folks didn't own any kind of electric fan, electric fans of any kind were just too expensive for the average family. Some homes (primarily those built in the thirties and forties) were equipped with what were called "whole-house" fans. These were a beautiful piece of ingenuity. In a central hallway of the house, you would see a large (about five feet) square opening in the ceiling with metal louvers. Above this opening a large belt driven fan was mounted, when you turned the fan on these louvers opened allowing hot air from the house to be drawn into the attic. This simple arrangement allow for two cooling affects to take place simultaneously. First, a Florida attic can easily reach temperatures in excess of 140° to 160°. This fan flushed out that supper hot attic air, replacing it with the air from inside the home. Second, and even neater, was that by keeping all the windows in the house CLOSED, except for one or two in the room(s) that you were occupying, you could create a delightful breeze blowing right on you. WHEN I moved into my present house it had a 'retro' fan mounted in a large window in the laundry room which at least served half the function of the whole-house fan. We used this fan with the kitchen and living room windows opened during the day and then only a single window in each bedroom was opened at night – it worked great! But, the new central air conditioning I later installed DOES work substantially better.

WISE OLD OWL

WISE OLD OWL... WHAT A HOOT!
WHO? WHO? TELL ME WHO SAID YOU WERE WISE.
I WISH TO FIND HIM; LAUGH IN HIS FACE
FOR HE'S AS DUMB AS YOU. WHO? WHO, TELL ME
WHO!

WISE OLD OWL! WHAT A HOOT! WHAT DO YOU KNOW?
YOU DON'T KNOW NOTHING! WHAT'S TWO AND TWO?

DO YOU KNOW ANYTHING? TWO PLUS TWO?
WHERE ARE YOU? DO YOU EVEN KNOW
WHAT DAY IT IS?

WISE OLD OWL... WHAT A HOOT! TELL ME WHO,
WHO SAID YOU WERE WISE!
IF YOU CAUGHT TWO FIELD MICE AND TWO CORN
SNAKES;
HOW MUCH WOULD THAT BE?
SEE! HE IS DUMB TO THINK YOU WISE.

WHAT? WHAT'S THAT YOU SAY?
TWO MICE AND TWO CORN SNAKES
EQUALS "FULL" FOR YOU AND YOUR FAMILY!
TWO PLUS ONE EQUALS "ALMOST FULL"
ONE PLUS ONE EQUALS "NOT ENOUGH"
AND TWO PLUS THREE EQUALS "TOO MUCH!"

AND THE PLACE YOU ARE AT?.......IS THE PLACE OF
PLENTIFUL FOOD AND SHELTER
FOR YOU AND YOUR FAMILY!

AND THE DAY? THE DAY IS "TODAY"
FOR YESTERDAY IS BEHIND YOU
AND YOU HAVE NO CONCERN
FOR TOMORROWS!

WISE OLD OWL! WHO? WHO? TELL ME WHO!
WHO SAID YOU WERE WISE? I WISH TO FIND HIM...........
AND SHAKE HIS HAND, FOR HE IS AS WISE AS YOU.
DAG

XV

OWLS

Raising Barn Owls and then a couple of Great Horn Owls is also something we tried once. Actually, Stevie Floyd did most of the 'raising' since we kept them at his house. The old Carlin house that you read about in Jupiter's history (it was the stopping point for the paddlewheel steamers and the Celestial Railroad) was still there when I was growing up. But it was abandoned and so it became our 'haunted house'. The place was huge and we used to love to sneak around in there in the middle of the night. Stevie (Floyd) and I once got some baby Barn Owls out of there. Yeah, that was a little scary too. Anyway, we fed and raised them to adults and later let them go. The Great Horn Owls came from a nest in the top of a giant pine tree out in the woods off Roebuck Road. We ended up building a huge 'flight' cage for them. Feeding them was an endless chore as they grew up. Shirley, Stevie's Mom, we always called her Shirley for some reason. I think because Stevie always called her "Shirley" and not "Mom." She was the only, and I do mean only adult we ever called by their 'first' name. You just did not do that when we were growing up! Anyway, Shirley sometimes stopped by Michael's Meat Market *[11]*. *{ Note: Michael's place was a little meat and grocery store that opened on Center Street about where the Circle-K is now. It was a great place to stop when I was* *walking home from School, which I did a lot of because I was always being sent to 'detention'. Michael slaughtered the cows, which were kept in a pasture that is now Penn Park, right there on the premises. We often watched as he lead a cow into a "neck bar" on the side of the store. And then watch him shoot them right between the eyes with a 22, or sometimes (he was a big man) just straddle the pen and swing a baseball bat down between his legs.}* Shirley brought home any outdated meat or chicken he might have. I think I might have brought down one or two of our chickens to feed them too. But 'our' chickens are another story! Mostly, Stevie and I caught mullet – which the owls weren't crazy about, or rabbit – which they love.

    We couldn't just go out and shoot rabbits on the Point by that time because by then there were other homes. Our solution was to 'shoot' them with palmetto darts. Palmetto darts were made by finding good flat Palmetto fronds and, using our pocket knives, trimming them down into the finest "darts" you ever saw. They were about a foot or so long overall with a very sharp point and a notch made a few inches back from the tip. They were shot using a loop of string tied to the end of a long piece of "Red Rubber" from a red rubber inner tube. "Red Rubber" was hard to find, but the 'red' was stretchier than regular old "black rubber." These things were very accurate, very quiet, and very deadly. We almost wiped out the entire population of rabbits from the Point feeding those owls. And, those owls grew huge, when the female sat on your arm, she measured about eighteen inches to the top of her head. The male measured almost twenty four inches. As they grew older we left their cage opened for longer and longer periods until they were completely free to come and go as they pleased. They came back to that cage for a very long time. I remember they used to scare the hell out of me at night when I was walking to or from Stevie's house along the trail we had through the woods between our houses. They would swoop down on you from behind your back and it was pitch black in those woods. They flew so quietly that you didn't hear them until they were right on top of you, and then, you'd 'hit the dirt' literally, because you thought they were going to try and 'take your head off'. I used to think they did it on purpose just to scare me, but, really it was because they knew me and figured I might have some rabbit for them.

THE EVENING

I LOVE TO WATCH THE EVENING COME,
TO KNOW MY DAY IS FINALLY DONE.
THAT SPECIAL TIME...
'TWIX DAY AND NIGHT.
WHEN SUN HAS SET,
BUT IT'S STILL LIGHT.

THE HERON,
ONE LAST FISH HE STALKS;
THEN OFF HE FLIES....
HIS USUAL 'SQUAWKS'.

THE DEW BEGINS TO SPREAD...
ITS BLANKET ON THE GRASS.
THE WATER STARTS TO CHANGE...
TO BLACKENED LIQUID GLASS.

A LATE SQUIRREL SCURRIES...
AS HE HURRIES
BACK THE PATH TO HOME.
THE DARKNESS WRAPS AROUND ME...
I'M ALONE.

THEN THE LIGHTS BEGIN TO GLOW
ALL ALONG THE RIVER.
EACH SENDS OUT A TINY SLIVER...
OF DANCING GOLD AND SILVER...
STRAIGHT TO ME.
REMINDS ME OF THE TINSEL
ON A CHRISTMAS MORNING TREE.

THEN,....I HEAR THE PHONE;
GUESS I'M NOT ALONE!
DAG

Gazabo II
(The Artist Studio)
(Pencil sketch)
<u>DAG</u>

XVI
PADDLE WHEELERS & RATTLESNAKES

Two of those paddlewheel steamers I mentioned earlier were scuttled up the river. You used to be able to see them up there. Even as I got older you could still see most of one hull and the brickwork holding up the boiler. Some say they were scuttled up there after they were no longer any good. But there was always a rumor that Mr. Flagler bought them and then had them scuttled so that people had to use his railroad. I don't know if that's true, but it sounds plausible to me! The hulls were up just past the "Hole-in-the-wall" of the river. That's what we always called that area where the river narrows very quickly because up until not too many years ago 'well, maybe twenty or thirty'. the trees and vegetation <u>did</u> grow all the way over from one side of the river to the other side. It was really beautiful the way it divided the 'upper river' and 'lower river,' The wide 'running around in' part of the river just abruptly stopped and then you went through this little hole in the solid wall of vegetation, when you passed through, you went into another world. Now you were in a true "wild and scenic" place. Looking back, I can only imagine what those tourist on the Jungle Cruise *{a tour boat to Trapper's – I'll get back to it later}* must have thought as they passed from the 'known' to the unknown!

Then there was the time that we heard that Trapper Nelson was buying rattlesnakes for the unheard of price of $1.00 a foot *{supposedly some serpentarium had contracted with him for the snakes}* . We immediately set about getting ready to "get rich." We gathered up our "tools" – a length of garden hose, a small funnel, and a can of gas – oh!, and a "snake pole" we had made up. It was a long pole with a wire loop at the end that we could pull tight after we got it over the snake's head. We knew that when it was really cold, the snakes crawled down to the bottom of the gopher holes to stay warm. And, we knew that when you got them to crawl out, they were so lethargic that you could practically pick them up with your bare hands and drop them in a crokersack. Of course, we weren't planing on doing "THAT!"– that is what the snake pole was for.

Getting them to come out of the gopher's hole was supposed to be easy too! First you slid the length of garden hose down the gopher hole; blew in the hose to get the sand out of it, then you flipped the hose around a few times to get the rattler to rattle. Putting your ear to the hose, you listened for that rattle – if you heard it, the rest was even easier! You put the funnel in the end of the hose, opened up your can of gas and started pouring. Jeez! They'd put you under the jail for that today! Well, anyway, after skipping school every cold morning for a month and checking out "Lord knows how many" gopher holes – we were batting zero. We did finally manage to practically step on two rattlers one day. And they <u>were</u> slow, what with it being so cold and all. So, getting our "snake pole" on them wasn't too tough. The hard part was then holding the snake on the ground with another stick while you worked the wire loop back up very close to his head – scary end! From there it was "into the crokersack." This again was the "hard part," while one person held open the sack, the other person dangled the snake down into the bottom – when that head was passing with inches of your hands – things got a little hairy. Once the snake was in the sack, you tried to loosen the loop while still holding the sack tight around the pole, and then get the pole out for the next "hunt." And, yes! The next one was even more fun – try to get a wiggling Rattlesnake into the bottom of a sack that already has a Rattler coiled up in the bottom. I wouldn't do it, I said that's what they made more crokersacks for! Well, to wrap this story up, we finally had our snakes and were ready to head for Trapper's, when we found out "he wasn't buying any snakes." Whether he was ever buying snakes for a 'buck a foot,' I don't know. But we sure didn't get rich!

I LEFT HER – BACK THERE!
(The selective memory of love and lust!)

BACK THERE, SOMEWHERE. THE GIRL OF MY DREAMS.
OR SO IT SEEMS... AT THE TIME!
I REMEMBER HER NAME, HER FACE... HER HAIR.
I REMEMBER EVERYTHING...
EXCEPT WHETHER WE EVER ACTUALLY KISSED.
I THINK WE WERE BOTH MAYBE FIVE OR SIX.
I LEFT HER – BACK THERE... SOMEWHERE.

MY FIRST REAL DATE
BEING SCARED, SCRUBBING CLEAN.
SMELLING LIKE THE BALM OF OLD SPICE.
I DON'T REMEMBER ANYTHING... ABOUT HER.
WHO SHE WAS, WHERE WE WENT.
I LEFT HER – BACK THERE... SOMEWHERE.

GETTING PAST 'FIRST BASE' YOU DO REMEMBER.
THE FIRST TIME YOU TOUCH A WOMEN'S BREAST
ISN'T SOMETHING YOU FORGET.
YES, THIRD BASE... I REMEMBER TOO!
BUT, I DON'T REMEMBER 'HER,' I REMEMBER 'IT.'
I LEFT HER – BACK THERE... SOMEWHERE.

AH, YES! 'THE HOME RUN.'
I REMEMBER <u>EVERYTHING</u> ABOUT 'HER'
AND VERY LITTLE ABOUT 'IT.'
I REMEMBER HER HAIR, HER EYES, HER FACE, HER
SMILE.

BUT I REALLY DON'T REMEMBER <u>ALL</u> THE REST!
ALL OF THAT IS SOMEHOW LOST.
BUT IT'S THERE – SOMEWHERE...
BACK THERE.

<u>DAG</u>

XVII

SCHOOL

Regular school itself was another neat thing back then; I liked school for pretty much the same reason I liked Sunday School! Truth be told, I did loved the summer better – even if I did have to work and had a lot of chores. We started working full time every summer at a fairly early age. In fact, I just got finished spending untold hours with the Social Security office (actually, my wife did! I got too pissed off at them) trying to figure out why my records didn't match their records. Seems I lied to get a 'work permit' when I was twelve, you had to be fourteen to get a 'work permit' so my age didn't match up. Heck, if I'd of known that was the problem to begin with, I could have just continued to lie about my age and retired two years earlier. Shoot!

Anyway, back to school! The entire school from first grade through twelfth grade was all in that one building on Loxahatchee Drive *[8]*. The elementary classes were on the first floor and the 'upper classes' were on the second floor. When you were in elementary school, it was always a great 'privilege' to be 'allowed' up on the second floor for some reason. The restrooms were located at the landing between floors so you often ran into one of the 'big' kids when you went to the bathroom. It really wasn't a problem though because it wasn't like you ran into a stranger or something, everyone knew everyone else's brothers and sisters, so they all

Shoes weren't a requirement when I was in Elementary School which was great because I hated shoes. Most of us had feet tough enough to walk across sand-spurs anyway. *{That reminds me, I gotta write about our sandspurs at some point too!}* It was pretty funny when the state or whoever started to require that "shoes be worn to school." Notice how I put that in quotes? Worn "to" school, not "in" school; there were literally hundreds of pairs of shoes sitting on the front steps of the schoolhouse every day. Sometimes we forgot to pick them up on the way home and that made us "in violation" the next day.

Knives were another "No Problem" in school. Shoot, you could have carried a "Twelve inch Jim Bowie Knife" on you and it probably wouldn't have raised an eye brow. We all (Yes! "All" meaning "boys" in this case) carried some kind of pocket knife by the time we were in third grade (in fact, many by the second grade), and we often played some form of "mumbly peg" at recess. I don't ever remember actually playing the game to its conclusion – pulling the "peg" [a stick, or kitchen match driven into the ground] it more often turned into a game of "stretch" or 'chicken'. Yes! As the names imply, they are two very distinctly different game. Teachers didn't usually frown on 'stretch' but 'chicken' was often forbidden or at least discouraged. Keep in mind that as we played these games, we were, as I said earlier, most often – BAREFOOT!

Fights, there were always fights; I probably had way

too many myself, at least in Elementary School. Yes, I lost more than a few, but I also won my share! Fighting with my brother all the time like I did, I got pretty good at it! School was good back then, big open (Remember? No Air Conditioning!) windows that you could stare out of and day dream – I probably did too much of that too!

Yes! I probably did way too much of "everything except school" at school. In fact, it was many, many years <u>after</u> school when I took my first real aptitude test and IQ test that I realized that I really wasn't "stupid" in school, I was just the world's greatest "slacker." But, enough of that – back to "school."

The school had a huge (for the size of the school) auditorium with a full orchestra pit and stage with theater draperies and all, the stage also served as a basketball court. They held all kinds of school and public events, including proms (though, Prom Night was more often held at the Civic Center on the beach) and graduations in that auditorium. More than one person went off the edge of that stage head first into that orchestra pit before they decided to close it (the pit) in. I remember as a kid, because I wasn't afraid of heights, I was often 'selected' (that meant getting out of class) to climb up in the rafters of the auditorium to 'fix the draperies,' or 'change out a light'. There is no way they would let a kid do that today!

As it happened, I was in the last graduating class to have students who started First Grade in the same building. There were six of us who had started First Grade together in that building and graduated together in that same building. Myself and Five girls: Sandi Lieb, Jennie Ledford, Linda Boales, Leslie Collier, and Janet Seabrook. There were others that may have stated in Second Grade or so, but it was just the six of us that 'made it all the way'. And, I have to say, I probably had a crush on each and every one of those girls at one time or another.

Unlike today's schools, the old Jupiter school is built up off the ground so there is a 'crawl space' under all of it. That space may be three or four feet high under the main parts of the school and you can stand up under the stage area, at least you could when I was little. If you go around in back of the school, you'll see the access holes. It's really neat under there, an almost pure white sand floor that reflects the light deep underneath the building and it was always very cool under there. Yes, you can tell that I have spent some time under there. Yep! That's the first place I got beyond 'first' base with a girl. Boy, I'm glad Mom can't read this! I don't think I'll talk about my first 'home run'.

MORNING'S FOGGY FINGERS
(On Cigarettes)

MORNING'S FOGGY FINGERS FUMBLE
FOR THE LITTLE WHITE STICKS.
MY LIGHTER'S LIT
BEFORE ITS REACHED MY LIPS.

I TAKE IN A GREAT DEEP BREATH
OF ITS ADDITORY DEATH,
ITS WARMTH AND SERENITY ENGULF ME
AS I HACK AND COUGH
TOWARD A SLOW DEATH...
BUT I'M HAPPY!

<u>DAG</u>

XVIII
SCHOOLS, MOM, & SMOKING

Speaking of my Mom, she was quite a lady. Everybody loved her, young and old alike. And could she ever cook! She could bake cakes, pies, cookies, and almost any other dessert you can think of; as well as any full course dinner you can think of, and I don't just mean "well," I mean fantastic! *{ In fact, to give you an idea just how good a cook she was – and, how good she was at "making something from nothing." She took on the job as head cook at the school when I was in elementary school. At that time, most of the kids "brown-bagged" it because, like today, the food wasn't that great. But, soon after she started cooking darn near every kid in the school started eating in the cafeteria. School lunch at that time was about twenty-five cent which included a pint of milk. SHE STARTED MAKING MONEY IN THE CAFETERIA (just like today's bureaucracy, that was a "NO, NO" – you weren't allowed to make money on school lunches).}*

Because she was such a good cook, every kid in town loved to get invited to "stay for dinner." She was just a sweetheart with anybody or anything, people and animals alike. And she was funny, she could keep you in stitches at times. In some ways she was just the opposite of my Dad. I never saw my Dad sleep past five – maybe six o'clock on New Years Day morning. And if he wasn't out at some required function, he was in bed by nine o'clock at the latest. Mom on the other hand could probably have slept till nine or ten every morning if it hadn't been for us kids; and, believe me, she was ALWAYS up for us kids. But she was also always up to all hours of the night, writing poetry or just "waiting up for one of us kids to get home." Sometimes I'd come home from a date at some 'ungodly' hour and we would stay up to an even later 'ungodly' hour talking. And, smoking, always her cigarettes not your own, and each of you might go through a whole pack while you sat there and talked about most anything. You really could talk to my Mom about anything and I 'do' mean 'anything'. And not just us kids, it seemed like anyone with a problem that needed someone to talk to, ended up at our house talking to my Mom. And again, that was 'young and old' alike. Yes, a lot of my friends and my brothers and sisters friends would sit and talk with my Mom for hours on end.

Another thing that was always funny with Mom, was how superstitious she was. She had been raised a devout Catholic. She even had the three oldest of us kids baptized in the Catholic church, even though we never went to a Catholic church. But the funny thing is, her superstitions out-weighed her religion at every turn. She tried to hide it, but she just couldn't and some of that superstition rubbed off on me. I think some probably rubbed off on my older siblings too, but they'd never admit as much. The one superstition that still 'touches' me at times is 'doors'. Yeah! Go figure! Mom had this thing that you should always 'go out' the same door you 'went in' and vice versa. To this day I'll find myself making a point of doing that. I will walk out the side door of my house to get the "Recycling Bins" and take them to the road. When I head back, the front door is right there in front of me. But, no! I'll walk all the way around to the side door just to 'go in' the same door I 'went out'. But don't tell anybody that, or my wife and employees will have a 'field day' of it.

Talking about my Mom and smoking reminded me of a few other "smoking" things. First, of course, was the fact that back in the fifties, I would venture to say that fifty percent or more of the adult population of this country probably smoked. And, in some localized areas, that percentage was probably much, much higher. I know I started smoking fairly regularly at about age twelve – I hate to admit that but it's true. My older brother and sister were heading down to Palm Beach High by that time so I could steal a cigarette or two from my Mom and "have a smoke" while I waited for the bus.

But long before that we were smoking acorn pipes (remember those?) filled with real tobacco if we could get our hands on some decent size cigarette butts. But, most often when we were out in the woods and came across some Rabbit Tobacco bushes, we would just decide it was time to find an oak tree with some good size acorns, make a pipe and stuff it with that Rabbit Tobacco, then "light up." Dam, that was some horrible tasting stuff – but, we kept doing it!

No! I finally "don't smoke!" I don't think of myself so much as an "ex" smoker as I do, "a smoker who isn't smoking." Even now if my Doctor told me I had a terminal illness, the first thing I would do would be to head for a Seven–Eleven and get some "smokes." *{ An interesting side note – to let you know how prevalent (and acceptable) smoking was until fairly recently. When I started going to Palm Beach Junior College (Now 'Community" College), smoking was permitted in many of my classrooms. It was at the teachers discretion. This continued when I later transferred to the University of Florida and, it was still the norm when I graduated in 1968.}* I don't know when the practice was stopped.

I SEE YOU!
(On having quit cigarettes)

YOU LITTLE BITCH, I SEE YOU!
OH! I'D SEE YOU IN ANY CROWD.
I CATCH THE SCENT OF YOU
AS SOON AS I ENTER ANY WHERE YOU ARE!

OH, YES! YOU SEDUCTIVE LITTLE BITCH,
I SEE YOU WITH ALL THOSE OTHERS.
I WATCH THE WAY THEY HOLD YOU
AND CARESS YOU--
AS I LONG TO DO.
THE WAY THEY BREATHE YOU IN--
AS I LONG TO DO!

I SEE YOUR GLOW,
I REMEMBER YOUR WARMTH,
YOUR TOUCH, YOUR SCENT.
OH, YES!
I REMEMBER EVERYTHING ABOUT YOU!

I WILL NEVER FORGET YOU.
HELL NO! YOU SEDUCTIVE LITTLE BITCH.
I WILL ALWAYS LONG TO HOLD YOU,
TO CARESS YOU,
TO BREATHE YOU IN TO ME.

YOU BITCH,
YOU'LL ALWAYS HAVE YOUR HOOKS IN ME.
IF YOU HAD YOUR WAY,
YOU'D HOLD ME
TILL MY DYING BREATH
BREATHING YOUR SEDUCTIVE DEATH.

DAG

EARLY IN THE EVENING

EARLY IN THE EVENING
AS THE SUN BEGINS TO FAD
AND THE SURFACE OF THE WATER
TAKES ON THAT GOLDEN SHADE.

I WATCH A SINGLE MULLET PLOP
HIS LAZY ARC OF THREE.
I SEE AN OSPREY WITH HIS MEAL
PERCHED HIGH UP IN A TREE.

I WATCH A LITTLE KINGFISHER,
SITTING ON A POLE.
HE SITS SO LONG AND ALL ALONE,
I'M SURE HE ACHES RIGHT TO THE BONE;

AS HE STUDIES THE WATERS
WITH THAT STATUETTE STARE
KNOWING HIS DINNER IS
DOWN THERE SOMEWHERE.

AND, THEN WITH A FLUTTER
HE DIVES WITH A SPLASH
AND OFF HE FLIES
WITH DINNER AT LAST.

DAG

IXX

CHICKENS

Almost the entire time that we lived on Pennock Point, we raised chickens. Dad also kept bees, but that's another story! It's the chickens that I hated. I love most every animal known to man with the exception of chickens! They're a big stinking 'pain-in-the-ass' in my book! The only thing good about a chicken is the eggs, but that's the one part of the chicken we didn't get a lot of because Mom could sell those to supplement the meager amount she was allotted to feed, cloth, and care for us. I don't know how she did it. We never went hungry because we ate a hell of a lot of fish and chicken. But the chicken was always the old hens that couldn't lay anymore, so they were only good for stewing. But Mom sure could make some good stews and pot-pies. We often had a garden going, and she used whatever she had to whip up a good meal. She also made a lot of our clothes, too; she was a great seamstress. But, back to those damn chickens. Several times a year, it was time to 'turn' the chickens; that meant getting new chicks to raise (Yeah, the little chicks <u>were</u> cute!) and then killing off the oldest ones.

Now there is nothing more fun than slaughtering chickens – and if you believe that, I've got a bridge to sell you! First, you get a big fire going and get a huge tub of water boiling, that's to dunk them in for pluckin' after you've chopped their heads off. Of course, it's already ninety-nine degrees outside so that fire and boiling water just really adds to the fun! Then you get to start the 'head chopping'. Usually you grab the chicken by the head and flop it over a big stump that you have set up for just that propose. The idea is to get its body to hang off the side of the stump so its neck is nice and stretched out, ready for the 'choppin' part. Someone's suppose to be holding the chicken at that point – often me! If you are 'holding' not 'chopping', you want to hang on to those feet more than anything so you don't get all scratched up. That means you're probably not holding down their wings like you should. So, when the head comes off, <u>you</u> are left holding this chicken by the legs and it's trying to "fly off into the wild blue yonder" – WITH NO HEAD! Needless to say, blood is flying everywhere, and you are covered in it! Along with all the wet sticking feathers you are covered in from the previous chicken you just plucked. There is no way around it. When you are plucking a hot wet chicken all those feathers stick to your 'pluckin' hand in big clumps and the only way to keep working is to shake them off. Because you're holding the chicken in the other hand, that means when you shake your 'pluckin' hand, feathers go flying up all over you. Yep! There's nothing like being covered from head to toe in hot chicken blood and feathers! Yeah! You can tell, I love chickens!

A SOFT SUMMER RAIN

THE SOFTNESS OF THE RAIN DROPS
THE SADNESS IN THEIR SOUND.
THE WHISPER OF THE TREE LEAVES
AS THEY FLUTTER TO THE GROUND.

THE FAR OFF DISTANT CRYING
OF A FLEDGLING LITTLE OWL.
THE HOOTING OF HIS MOTHER
SAYING, "ALRIGHT, QUIET NOW!"

CRICKETS START TO CHIRP
TO THE SOUND OF A WHIP-POOR-WILL.
A RACCOON FAMILY ARGUES
IN THEIR USUAL HIGH PITCHED SHRILL.

A LAST DOVE CHORTLES
TO THE BACKUP SOUNDS OF QUAIL,
AND SOMEONE ROILS THE HERON
WHO THEN FLYS OFF WITH A WAIL.

THE SOFTNESS OF THE RAIN DROPS
THE SADNESS IN THEIR SOUND.
THE WHISPER OF THE TREE LEAVES
AS THEY FLUTTER TO THE GROUND.

DAG

XX

TRAPPER'S AND THE JUNGLE CRUISE

Back to some of the other more interesting (and fun) things. The Jungle Cruise that I mentioned earlier was a tourist attraction out of Riviera Beach. It used to bring tourist up to Trapper Nelson's place almost every day during the winter season. *{ The Jungle Cruise boat was a beautiful mahogany hulled boat, probably thirty-five to forty feet long, that looked just like an "African Queen" you might see on the Nile River. It had a draft of four feet (or more, depending on its load) which gives you an idea of just how deep the river was at that time.}* We used to try and 'time' our water skiing to their passing by the Point. We found that if we skied up next to them, we could often talk one of the tourist into passing us a soda. Getting a soda was a real treat, but getting the tourist to give it to you was really the best part.

We often skied all the way up to Trapper Nelson's, *{Note: Just not when the Jungle Cruise was headed there – that would have pissed off Trapper. And, pissing off Trapper is not something you wanted to do because once he banned you from coming to his place, that was it! You were probably never going to be invited back.}* There weren't a lot of boats on the river at the time – good thing though! If you met a boat coming the other way while you were in the narrowest, winding parts of the upper river, you often found yourself thrown up into those mangroves. Of course, a lot of times, if you were driving the boat, you were trying to throw the skier off anyway – just for the fun of it! I remember skiing up the river one day and as I swung out wide on the skis, I hit a good size alligator. It was like hitting a big log in the river. It scared the hell out of both of us, but, I'm sure, 'me' more than the 'gator'. I went flying up in the air, but having seen what I'd hit, I wasn't about to fall in. I still don't know how I managed to "land on my feet" and stay on those skis, but I did!

Trapper Nelson's was always a fun place. He really did like kids, as long as we didn't cause trouble or bother his 'paying' clientele – the tourist. When we were old enough to run the "motorboat." I say "motorboat" because I think we were allowed to take a "rowboat" out damn near as soon as we could swim. Maybe a little older than that! We could all swim by time we were one or two years old. But, anyway, we'd take the boat to Trapper's. Just as often, I would ride our horse up there, sometimes with Sandi Lieb – she had a huge horse she called "Big Red" – but, most often, I would just ride up there myself for 'something to do'. Trapper had a big rope swing that we all used to love to swing on. Sometimes after a good rain, the water was so clear you could actually put a dive mask on and dive down amongst the cypress tree roots. Fun, but a little scary too! I think most of the tourist thought we were some kinda 'half-wild' natives ("Native" as in Indians) or something. No shoes, no shirts, ragged baggy dirty shorts at best, and our skin so tan we didn't look like "white people," at least not "white people" like the northern tourist. But we had as much fun with them as they did with us! Just like you see in the movies of a cruise ship pulling into a foreign port, we'd do most anything for a coke, candy, or coin.

TINY WHITE LIGHTS

TINY WHITE LIGHTS
IN A BRIGHT NIGHT'S SKY.
JUST TINY WHITE LIGHTS
AS A PLANE FLIES BY.

GOING HERE OR THERE,
OR WHO KNOWS WHERE.
JUST TINY WHITE LIGHTS
IN A BRIGHT NIGHT'S SKY.

LIKE A WHOLE TINY TOWN
IN A THIN TIN CAN,
GOING HERE OR THERE,
OR WHO KNOWS WHERE.

JUST TINY WHITE LIGHTS
IN A BRIGHT NIGHT'S SKY.
AN ENTIRE TINY TOWN
IN A THIN TIN CAN

WITH TINY WHITE LIGHTS
AGAINST A BRIGHT NIGHT'S SKY.
GOING HERE OR THERE,
OR WHO KNOWS WHERE.

<u>DAG</u>

XXI
MODES OF TRANSPORTATION

Getting around town as a kid often depended on where you were trying to get to, and when you were trying to get there. If it was on the water, no problem, you just jumped in you boat. We took our boats everywhere; we'd have taken them to school if we could. Next, of course, came your bicycle. We all rode our bicycles everywhere we couldn't get by boat. In Elementary School, I rode my bike most days just because I could get there earlier and have more fun before school started. We even rode and (mostly) walked our bikes to Trapper's – riding a bike on pure white, soft sugar sand is not easy! I rode our horse a lot too, but that was just in the woods mostly. Another neat way to get around was to 'hitch a ride' on the milk truck. Ted Ledford had the milk route in our area. So, you could always get up early enough to catch him and he'd give you a ride anywhere on his route. All you had to do was ride along and help out with the deliveries on the way. It was fun and it was always cool { *literally – 'cool'*} riding in the back of his milk truck what with all the ice packed backed there. The 'down side' was, riding to your destination could sometimes be a very long ways around.

Depending on the time of day, you might just start walking, because if anyone, and I do mean 'anyone' saw you walking they would stop and give you a ride. Everyone in the entire area knew everyone else and their kids, so they'd always give you a ride. But you did have to watch the time of day. I could start walking home from the School (on Loxahatchee Drive) and get all the way home (on Pennock Point) and never have seen a single car. It seems I did that a lot in my 'middle school' years because I was always being sent to detention hall which of course, meant you missed your bus. To understand just how small this area was at that time. Consider that up through the middle fifties, there were probably not more than three hundred to three hundred and fifty families living in the entire area between what is now PGA Boulevard (it wasn't there then) and Hobe Sound. Yes, that is excluding the "Winter Residents" which don't count!

XXII

U. S. HWY. #1 & LIGHTHOUSE RESTAURANT

U.S. Hwy. #1 was practically empty, especially during the summer. How empty you might ask? Well, the Mayos' had a gas station on the corner of U.S. #1 and State Road 707 (the road that turns into Beach Road) right across the street from the Lighthouse restaurant – about where the Walgreens is now. But the roads didn't run like they are now and, of course, they were much narrower. Anyway, Bo Mayo had a small plane. Often he would land the plane on U.S. #1 and keep it at the garage. When he was ready to takeoff, he would have his brother Glynn (the local constable – Glynn's a whole other story I hope to get too) drive up to the top of the hill (about where Tequesta Drive Traffic light is now) and flash his headlights if a car <u>was</u> coming which was rare. When it was clear, Bo took off in his plane.

Since I'm on the subject of U.S. #1, I might as well tell you about the Lighthouse Restaurant. I don't remember it being there when I was real, real little; but it has been there a very long time. It was a true Truck Stop, the kind of place my Dad wouldn't even let my older sister go into by herself. The south end of the building behind the gas station had 'rooms' the truckers could rent. They wouldn't let us go back there as a kid. There was a bathroom with showers so the truckers could clean up and rent a 'bed' for the night. I say "rooms" and "bed" because the rooms <u>were</u> the size of a bed. Each space was about four feet by seven feet, just enough for a cot size bed and a foot of space to get into it. But, 'rumor' has it, that place served as a brothel more than a place to sleep! Yes, you can tell, I <u>had</u> been back there. But NOT because it was a brothel!

The restaurant wasn't much to talk about either. It was fairly small, just a straight counter looking into the kitchen and then a few tables and booths. It had an open rafter ceiling. Two things I still remember. One, was sitting in one of those booths one night, and the owner of the place comes out with his 22 and starts shooting the rats up in the rafters. Yes, true story! The other time I was sitting at the counter when a trucker came in and ordered a bowl of chili and there was a giant roach in it. You wouldn't have known except for seeing these two 'tomato paste' covered antenna wiggling around in the air. The trucker didn't say a word, he just took that bowl of chili in his hand, and with a quick flip, flipped it right up side down on the counter – and then, walked out!

But growing up, the Lighthouse restaurant and its parking lot was 'the place in town' for us as teenagers. At that time all the High School grades hung out together. There just weren't enough teenagers to break into 'clicks' or anything like that, so if you "went to school on the 'second' floor" you were all part of the same crowd. Often, we would be 'hanging out' in the Lighthouse parking lot and all decide to 'head for the beach' and have a party. Beach Road (707) at the time headed straight from U.S. #1, across 'Cato's Bridge' and right up onto the dune-line. From there it turned north and headed all the way up Jupiter Island right on the dune-line.

WHERE HAVE YOU BEEN?
(Little girls grow up.)

YOU WERE A PLAYMATE
WHEN WE WERE JUST SIX.
PLAYING "HORSEY" AND OTHER
"LITTLE KIDS" GAMES.

NOW TURNING SIXTEEN,
I SEE YOU OF LATE
AND **'WOW'** HOW I WISH
YOU WERE STILL MY PLAYMATE.

I THINK I'M IN LOVE
I THINK I CAN SAY
OH HOW I WISH,
THAT WE COULD STILL PLAY

"HORSEY" AND OTHER
"LITTLE KIDS" GAMES.
OH HOW I WISH,
THAT WE COULD STILL PLAY

DAG

XXIII

BEACH ROAD & FRUIT FIGHTS

Today, when you are heading up Jupiter Island and the road makes a hard ninety degree turn east and then a hard ninety degrees back north, from that point south is where the original Beach Road used to be. About the time I got to High School (1960±), the original road was barricaded at "Blowing Rocks Park" and the road from there up to the ninety degree turns was moved down to its present location. And then, I think some time in the late sixties, the rest of the road was move down to where you see it today.

But, back to 'then' when the road was right on the beach and so narrow it was often hard to pass another car on it. There were many nights that I was called on to get my Dad's four-wheel drive Jeep and help pull some kid's car off the beach after he failed to make that corner, or he'd just gotten too close to the edge and one wheel slipped off. And, it was amazing how many times <u>it was the same kid!</u> (Yeah! You know who you are!) Anyway, heading over to the beach, when you got across Cato's Bridge, right before the road turned north, there was a little shellrock parking area cut into the middle of the palmettos. We called that spot the "finger bowl." No, I have 'no idea' how it got that name, but that's what we called it. If you were going to 'make out' with a date, that's where you parked. If you were 'just on a date' and didn't want to look too 'forward' you just parked on the main beach road. Further up the road just before Blowing Rocks there was another little spot down by the intracoastal; there was an old basketball hoop down there, so naturally we called that spot the 'basketball court'. When you were a little more 'serious,' that's where you 'parked'. If we were all just hanging out, we just parked along the road, standing around with our radios blasting. If it was a cool night, or "we just felt like it," we gathered up a bunch of driftwood and got a fire going. Sometimes we camped out right there on the beach, but we usually planned for that and brought food and something to sleep on! There were only two small beach houses on that entire stretch of road from the bridge to past Blowing Rocks, both right up near the road. *{Note: Years later, about 1969, after I got out of collage (and Beach Road had been move down from the dune line); I manage to rent each of those places. The first one as a bachelor and the second one when I first got married. My rent was $150 a month and that was for years and years, even long after the rents for such a place were $1500 or more. There were still no high-rise condominiums on the island yet and you could still run beach buggies on the beach. Yes, I am a lucky guy! And, yes, I know, if those places were still there, the rents would be $15,000 A WEEK now!}*

Another thing that used to happen along that road was the annual "Fruit Fight" between the Seniors and the Underclassmen. We would spend the entire week before the fight collecting as much rotten fruit (mostly grapefruit, oranges, and tomatoes) as we could get our hands on in preparation for that night. In fact, it wasn't really all rotten, it was any fruit we could "beg, borrow, or steal." And, yeah, we did steal a lot of it! The Seniors always tried to kidnap the 'ring leaders' of the Underclassmen, so they couldn't make it to the fight. This was 'during school,' but the school never really interfered with the 'goings on'. And, yes, I was generally considered a "ringleader." I'm sure primarily because I had my Dad's old Jeep pickup, and we had it loaded down with fruit. A few years after my Senior year, they banned "Fruit Fights" when someone came up with the bright idea of making a giant slingshot out of old inner-tubes and mounting it on a truck. The first guy hit went to the hospital; he ended up being all right but that was the end of "Fruit Fights."

ALL THE WORLD

(My first ever poem – at least what I remember of it)
Hey! I know, It's a little "over the top" But
this was the sixties, we were in the middle of a space race.
Everything was a little over the top and kinda 'out of this world'.
BESIDES, "I WAS IN LOVE!"

IF ALL THE WORLD WERE BUT A DROP...
OF WATER 'PON A LEAF...
HUNG TO A TWIG...
UPON A BRANCH
HUNG TO A TREE...
UPON AN ISLE...
AMID AN INFINITE SEA.

MY LOVE FOR YOU WOULD BE
AS HUGE, AS GIGANTIC, AS IMMENSE
AS ALL THAT WORLD.
AND YET, AS USELESS IN ITS NEED BY THEE
AS THAT DROP IS TO THAT SEA.

DAG

XXIV
GLYNN MAYO & DRIVE-THRU BARS

This is probably a good time to bring Glynn Mayo back up. As I mentioned earlier, he was "The Police Force" for the entire area. They have named a section of Alternate A1A for him. But in my mind, he deserves a statue. That man, single handedly, did more to get a "hell of a lot of" kids back on the "straight and narrow" than any other man I know. Yes, myself included! Many times he would find one of us so drunk we didn't know what was happening, and he would either drive us home to our parents or, if he thought we could drive at all, have us follow him to our homes. That's not "all" he did for us, that's just "all" I'm telling. The guy was great with us kids! He did have a way to get his kicks though! He liked driving up Beach Road with his lights out, he drove an old Station wagon, not a Police Car and he seemed to delight in sneaking up on us when we were 'parked'. Here you've got the windows all steamed up, and this '10,000 watt' flashlight comes shining in your window. Yes! He probably did 'save' more than one girl that way, but I'm a guy! Glynn knew every hiding spot and parking spot in town because he'd "been there" and "done that." He grew up here too!

Talking about Glynn and the "law" at that time, it was not illegal to "drink and drive." You did have to be twenty-one, but that was it. Which brings up another interesting note — "Drive-thru Windows." Yes! The first "Drive-thru" in Jupiter was not the McDonalds or Burger King – it was Glens Bar (different "Glynn.") A part of that Bar (the building) is still located on the Southeast corner of the intersection of Center Street and Alt. A1A. *{ Note: They tore most of the building down for the road widening.}* It had a "Drive-thru Window, " as long as the driver was twenty-one, he (she) could order any (and as many drink(s) as they wanted. And, we did! Off we'd go with our rum & cokes, or seven & seven's, or whatever in our plastic "to go" cups. In fact, even when we started going to bars and nightclubs, we often had our drinks poured into "to go" cups at closing time and/or if we were headed for another bar.

Cattails and Ducks
(Pencil sketch)
DAG

DAMSELS AND DRAGONS

NO FAIRY CAME...BUT A PRINCE,
IN TARNISHED ARMOR TOO!
HE ONCE WAS BRIGHT AND SHINY NEW
BUT AGE HAS DULLED HIS LUSTER.

FAIR DAMSEL'S DRAGONS HE ONCE SLEW
AND PUT HER FEARS TO REST.
BUT NOW SHE KNOWS HIS SECRETS THROUGH,
HIS STRENGTHS AND WEAKNESS TOO!

BUT EVEN THEN, SHE KNOWS THAT WHEN
A DRAGONS HEAD DOES RAISE.
HER PRINCE WILL BE AS SHE WILL SEE
WITH ALL THE STRENGTH HE MUSTERS
TO SLEW THE DRAGONS OF HER MIND AND
PUT IT ALL AT EASE.

BUT NOW, SHE SEES THE HELP HE NEEDS
TO PUT THE DRAGONS DOWN...
AND BY HIS SIDE THEY BOTH DO STRIDE
TO FIGHT THEIR BATTLES THROUGH.

THE WOUNDS OF ONE, THE OTHER'S PRIDE
FROM BATTLES FOUGHT AND WON.
IN LOVE THEY GO; THE BATTLES BLOW,
WITH STRENGTH IN EACH THE OTHER'S GLOW.

<u>DAG</u>

XXV
GROWTH OF AREA AND ME

Things in Jupiter really started to "blow wide open" in the late fifties and early sixties. The Turnpike was finished, Pratt and Whitney Aircraft Plant opened and Charlie Martin and the gang had begun developing all of Tequesta and Jupiter Inlet Beach Colony.

When I was in the seventh grade, there were just two students in the Senior Class. *{Note: Some of that was due to parents sending their kids to Palm Beach High at the time to better prepare for a college education. My older brother and sister went to Palm Beach High – at Mom and Dad's insistence, not theirs. Yes! Burt Reynolds had the privilege of going to school with my siblings.}* In fact, this was the single biggest change of my school life. Up until that time I was always "the little brother" at school. And, as I got a little older, I was hesitant to "try anything" for fear my siblings would not approve – or worse, tell our Dad. But, by eighth grade, it was just me – no more "Big Siblings" checking on, and reporting on, me! Of course, after that many years of having them "always there," it took some getting used to. But I did manage to "spread my wings."

{In fact, an interesting side note! Here I am sixty years old and my older sister who is a Jupiter School librarian, just

called me to say that she had been looking at a yearbook from my senior year and just found out that I had been president of the Student Council. We both got a kick out of how little we really know about each other.}

Another neat thing that happened related to our high school was the opening of the Colony Restaurant (on the S.E. corner of Loxahatchee Drive and Indiantown Road) about the time I became an "Upper Classmen." Because, "Upper Classmen" could go off campus for lunch. Anyway, by the time I graduated in 1963, there were fifty or more of us in the graduating class. Yes, a BIG change!

In fact, the school got so much bigger each year that they "Upped by one year," the grade that was allowed to go off campus for lunch; until by my senior year, when only Seniors could go to the Colony. *{Note: They also built a new Elementary School about the time I was moving "Up Stairs" into High School.*

Personally, I found it a little tough and intimidating when all these seemingly wealthy and sophisticated kids started to 'take over my world'. I was used to all of us 'being in the same boat'. We didn't have any money or fancy clothes, but neither did any of our peers. Suddenly there were kids that were stylish and drove their own cars. They had swimming pools (something unheard of before that) and new boats. It was hard not to feel somehow inferior to all that, but I managed. I think my father's status helped. Even though we weren't wealthy, my father was a very bright, well educated man with a lot of respect in the community and that somehow gave credence to my own "self worth." The fact that we lived on the river was a 'big thing' by that time and that helped even if you did have to chase the chickens away and step around the chicken shit when you had someone over. Besides, at that time my Dad still always had the biggest boats and as long as I kept gas in them, I could use them. Boy, did we have some great times on his boats! Skiing in the ocean is a blast! And big boats have coolers and radios and BEDS. Whoops, that may have been the "home run," sorry about that Mom!

It was really only after I had graduated from high school that I learned how shy I really was. Up until then I had never been the "new kid on the block" so I was always welcoming people into "my world." I always knew I was shy around girls, but in high school there were enough opportunities for a girl to get to know "me," first. With that level of comfort, I could then proceed to get to know "her." I had never "Gone Steady" with anyone; there had been lots of girls I liked, but none I really "LOVED." Once I was out on my own, I was lost!

When I was going to Palm Beach Junior (now "Community") College I couldn't meet anyone new – I was too shy and I didn't know how. I still remember years later, getting to know some people who had been at JC (Junior College) with me, they all said that they had always thought I was "stuck up" when I was going to JC. That is the way my shyness came across – learning that really hurt! I have to admit that I had begun trying to find courage in a bottle at that point and was drinking entirely too much.

I did date a lot of girls I already knew and/or that one of my friends set me up with. I remember I managed to finally get up the courage to ask one particular girl out. My desire to get to know her finally over came my fears. Actually, she was someone from my high school – just not my class – so I had never actually gotten to know her. She had intrigued me from the first time I saw her. *{Yes, you are astute in noticing that I am leaving out 'names' at this point in my story. I am protecting the _____? Well, you fill in the blank.* Looking back, I probably didn't make such a great first impression what with too much drinking and smoking. All I know is that each time she said, "yes" to another date I felt more and more sure that she was "the one." And, when she finally said, "no," I was devastated.

I searched for years and never found anyone like her. I remember when I finally got up to the University of Florida, I had an opportunity to go out to Lake Tahoe (Nevada) for a summer job. I almost didn't come back to college because I met a "look alike" to my first love. I didn't love this girl, but we had a blast. Having lived in Lake Tahoe all her life, she knew what 'trails to hike' and 'waterfalls' to see that no regular 'tourist' would ever get to see. And, this was the 'Sixties," so it was great to have a chance to go to San Francisco and "see where it all began."

When I finally did get back to Gainesville and try to

wrap up this 'getting a Degree' thing, I stumbled across the girl I was to later marry. "Stumble" comes pretty close to describing how it all "went down." It was like this, I was just coming out of the bookstore where I had bought probably nothing – having used the place as an excuse to park my car or some such thing. Anyway, this "Drop Dead Gorgeous Blond" walks up to me and says, "You don't remember me, do you?" Well all I can say is, "I SURE AS HELL WANTED TO REMEMBER HER!" But, 'I didn't have a clue!' Seems we both went to Jupiter High – I was just three years ahead of her. But, I don't think I even remember her saying that at the time. Truth was I didn't remember much of anything she said. I was too busy tripping over my tongue and slaughtering my ability to say anything. Hey, how often did you have a beautiful blond walk up to you?

Anyway, to make this whole story a little shorter. She had told me her name – which I didn't remember! She had told me where she lived – which I didn't remember! All I do remember is that I finally got up the nerve to ask her if she would like to go get a cup of coffee. All I heard was NO! She said she had a 'Class' to get to – I had never had a 'Class" stop me from doing anything. So I naturally took that to mean, "Oh no! I was JUST saying, 'Hi!' I don't want to have anything to do with you!" So that was the end of that!

A number of years later, I'm back in dear 'ol Jupiter – AND, I've got my Degree! Every night after 'regular' work I would go work on my sailboat and then, 'knock-off' about ten or eleven and head down to HoJo's (Remember? Howard Johnson's!) to get something to eat. 'Lo and behold' she – Yes! "SHE" as in the "Drop Dead Gorgeous" from Gainesville "SHE" – has taken a summer job there.

Again, I have to be honest here, and tell you – I didn't recognize her as the same girl. In my defense, do any of you remember what the sixties 'HoJo' uniform (brownish, with the matching hair net) looked like? Think "BROWNISH!" That's what they looked like!

So, kinda on a dare (I often went to HoJo's with another guy that also had a sailboat – he 'dared me') and, wondering what she might look like 'out of that uniform' (No, not that way! Wearing something 'other than' that uniform). I (again) got up the nerve to ask her out and the rest is history – thirty some years later and she's still gorgeous.

HAND SAWS

I MISS THE SOUND OF THE SAW.
NO! NOT THE WHIRLING, WHINING
EAR DRUM SPLITTING SCREAMING
OF SOME MOTOR DRIVEN CIRCLE SAW!

I MISS THE SOUND OF A SHINY
SHARP TOOTHED HAND SAW
DRAWN BY THE STRONG STRAIGHT ARM
OF AN OLD CARPENTER.

FROM SIX POINT TO SIXTEEN
AND EVERYTHING IN BETWEEN!
BASE TO SOPRANO
EACH SINGS ITS OWN SONG...
WHEN DRAWN BY THE STRONG STRAIGHT ARM
OF AN OLD CARPENTER.

DAG

XXVI
GROWTH OF AREA – CHANGES

Yes, there were a lot of changes in Jupiter in a very short time. Some of us that have been here awhile joke that you can tell how long someone has been here by asking them where the first bowling ally was. There is one off Indiantown Road now and a lot of people who have been here a little while would say that the 'first' one was over where Sunshine Plumbing is now, right behind Dune Dog Cafe. But the first bowling ally was at the north end of Village Square Shopping Center. It was built as a bowling ally right at the time the shopping center was built (I am guessing that was right around 1959). In fact, the south end of the shopping center which opened as a Piggly Wiggly (our first real grocery store), later (sometime in the middle to late sixties) housed our first real theater. Shortly thereafter another theater opened at the old shopping center (now gone) on the north side of Tequesta Drive; *{ Note: As it happens, the area still wasn't big enough to support two theaters so they both ended up closing. Now look, there must be eight or ten theaters!}*

During the early sixties I had several friends who worked at that Piggly Wiggly, so, on a few occasions, we had more beer and cigarettes than we knew what to do with. Piggly Wiggly also hired five or six us to do inventory twice each year. We were paid fifty dollars for a weekend taking the inventory at the five stores they had between here and Riviera Beach. At the time, fifty bucks was a whole heck of a lot of money to earn in just one weekend. It was at this time (early sixties) that the same group of us spent a lot of time camping and hunting out by Lainhart's dam. One of those friends, Chuck Griffin and his family lived right there near the creek. We spent hours and hours rebuilding that dam in order to keep the water level high at our 'swimming hole' further up stream. We also spent days at a time out there, camping, exploring, and (pretending we were) hunting. *NOTE: When the first "edition" of this book (the Fat Pamphlet) came out, I got an E-mail from Kristl Bogue (from my class of '63). She said that no one ever believed her when she describe wading through muck up to your knees – just to go swimming.. And, don't forget, we never went swimming without first throwing a few M-80's or Cherrybombs in under the cypress roots to scare away the water moccasin – and any alligators if they happened to be around. Of course, we always told the girls we only did that for their benefit. Yeah! Right! Kristl also said that people seemed to doubt her when she described going hunting for rattlesnakes – AS A DATE! But it's true!*

Change was everywhere and in everything during this time period. Not just the phenomenal changes in Jupiter what with all the new roads, new bridges, and new developments – but also, the phenomenal changes in our technology. I know that they were working a railroad line across the country more than a hundred years earlier and the entire Industrial

Revolution had come and gone. We had automobiles, electric power, and airplanes. Heck, my own house built in 1925 had a beautiful full bathroom, kitchen and electric lights in every room. And it was what, just a couple years after that, that Charlie Lindbergh made his historic flight? The point I am trying to make is that, yes we had some great technology going on – but, you'd have thought we were in the Dark Ages compared with today.

For example, I still remember walking into my Dad's office and watching Johnny Lieb (the office manager) adding up a column of numbers on the best thing available at the time – a hand operated adding machine. This one was the "portable desk top model," it probably weighed close to thirty pounds. It looked more like a slot machine than an adding machine. Anyway, you mechanically (NOT, electrically) punched each individual number, decimal point, and cents into it; and then pulled the big lever on the side to MECHANICALLY add that amount to the previous amount. Do you remember what it took to calculate the 'Square Root' of a number – especially a large number? Now, there is a little credit card size calculator sitting in my pocket as I type this (on my notebook size computer) that can do all of that and more. Yeah ! Pretty amazing!

To make copies of documents you had to plan ahead, putting carbon paper between several sheets of paper before you put them into your typewriter. Yes, that's where the phrase, "carbon copy" came from. I do remember their (the office's) first 'real' copier though – it consisted of a roll of photo sensitive paper and a special light. By shining the light through the original, it exposed the photo paper underneath creating a very crude copy for your records.

Even the tools used in residential construction at the time were all hand tools. Yes, we had long ago built the Empire State Building, the Panama Canal, and more recently, some of the best fighting equipment in the world. But we still didn't have small affordable power tools on home building jobs. To drill a hole through concrete, we were still using a star-bit (like a chisel with a star shaped end) and hammer. All wood was cut by hand and all nails were hammered in with a hammer, even concrete nails.

In truth, everything about the world – at least locally – was a softer, quieter sound. With no Air Conditioning, everyone's windows were wide open and with all the construction around then you would have thought the noise would be horrible, but it wasn't. You didn't hear the constant sounds of compressors and power equipment. You heard the sound of heavier hammers driving in bigger nails during the framing stages and lighter hammers driving in smaller nails during the finishing stages. This was true of the sounds of the saws also, bigger toothed saws cut bigger lumber, finer tooth saws cut finer woods. You could actually tell by the sound what was being cut.

I TOOK A WALK

I TOOK A WALK ON OUR BEACH LAST NIGHT
THE MOON, THE STARS, THAT OCEAN —
"WHAT A SIGHT!"

A LATE SUMMER'S RAIN HAD JUST COME...
AND GONE AS QUICK.
SHOWN ITS BIT OF FURRY...
AND THEN IT WENT —
LEAVING THE SKY TO DO ITS THING.

THE SAND WAS COLD... AND WET
BENEATH MY FEET, THE AIR
WAS CLEAR AND CLEAN.
THE ONLY SOUND —
THE SEA.

THE SANDPIPERS AND SEAGULLS HAD
GONE HOME FOR THE NIGHT. JUST I, ALONE
WITH THE GHOST CRABS... AND OTHERS
THAT ROAM IN THE NIGHT.

BUT ALONE I WAS NOT, FOR
ONE IS NEVER ALONE ON A WALK
ON THE BEACH. I ALWAYS
HAVE MY THOUGHTS.

AND WHO AM I THINKING OF...?
DID YOU ENJOY
OUR WALK ON THE
BEACH LAST LIGHT?

DAG

XXVII

U. S. #1 AND A1A BRIDGES

Next time you are in a boat, look at the little pieces of the previous U.S. #1 and Alternate A1A *{Note: we called it Damon's bridge}* bridges that have been left – you are also looking at major changes in our town. The old U.S. #1 road and it's bridge were very low so that when you went across it, you looked right at the old Coast Guard Barracks; in fact, you almost looked 'up,' not 'down' like you do today. And, when you were headed south across that bridge, you didn't go straight past the Historical Museum and Welcome Center (which weren't there) and continue south like you do today. No, U.S. #1 and A1A were one and the same road at that time. U.S. #1 did not go straight south, it curved east, following the same route as old A1A up to the beach through Juno, and then back to its present location where A1A forks off U.S. #1 now, at the south end of Juno. *{I know, I find it hard to believe myself – that the intersection we see today at U.S.#1 and Indiantown Road did not exist in the late fifties. Indiantown Road did not cross the Intracoastal Waterway or even cross the rail road tracks at that time. And, going west wasn't much better, Indiantown Road was only paved to the Center Street intersection.}*

It was at that turn onto the U.S. #1 bridge (headed back north) that my Mom and older sister had their strange accident. They were coming back from Riviera Beach in our Willey's Jeep Station wagon (Yes! The kind we always owned) when Mom went to press the breaks for the turn on to the bridge – one wheel locked up and the other three did nothing. Needless to say, the Jeep started rolling over. It seems someone had topped the break fluid reservoir with the wrong fluid. A few things to note about all this. At that time all payrolls were all cash, not checks like today. Johnny Lieb, Dad's office manager would call down to the bank in Riviera Beach and give them the total pay, right down to the penny, for each man. The bank then gave you the exact amount of pennies, nickels, dimes, dollars, etc. that were needed to make up each mans 'pay envelope'. Mom had all that cash with her as well as two weeks worth of groceries, two fifty pound bags of chicken feed, and, because of a pending party, several wood cases of cokes in the old glass bottles. When they flipped, the first thing that happened was that the two bags of chicken feed burst open, and all the coke bottles exploded. Mom and my sister both said they had the same reaction as the Jeep came to rest on its side. Their eyes were closed, they were covered in chicken feed, and they are both thinking that what they feel running down their bodies is the other one's blood. It was that warm coke from all those bottles, and it felt just like blood! They were both badly shaken-up but otherwise okay. It was then that Mom remembered the money. It was in a zipped bank bag so it didn't fly everywhere, but she still was scared to death just having it! I'm guessing it was 1957 or '58 when all this happened, and as I said, there were few 'strangers' around; but 'lo and behold,' it is a complete stranger that is the first to come by. The first thing Mom does, is blurt out that she has all this cash money. I think the accident had her brain rattled, but everything worked out all right, and the guy drove them to Dad's office.

Also at that time, what is now called 'Alternate' A1A did not exist; there was just Old Dixie Highway. Heading south across the (now) 'Alternate' A1A bridge, you could cross the railroad tracks at Center Street or continue past the (then) railroad station to where Old Dixie crossed the tracks at Old Beach Road (which is just south of Bell's Trailer Park and right across the railroad tracks from the Old Dixie Cafe). *{Note: Old Jupiter Beach Road was (even before my time) the road that would have taken you over to DuBois Park and the beach – because even US. Hwy. #1 wasn't there yet!}* Over on the west side of the tracks, Old Dixie continued south until well past (what is now) the Admiral's Cove area before crossing again to the east side of the tracks. In fact, it was just after you crossed back to the east side of the railroad tracks that you crossed a small concrete bridge with high arching sides that we called "Rainbow Bridge."

When we were very little "Rainbow Bridge" was that magic spot where if you were with a girl when you crossed it, you could kiss her. Yes! I will never forget that bridge, I hated to see it come down. kinda like a "Ba-diddle," remember those? When you met another car coming at you with one headlight, it meant you could kiss your date! Yes, those were fun times. And, yeah! If that game's still around today – the rules have probably changed. Besides, how many headlights do you see burned out today compared to back then? But back to the Alternate A1A (Previously Old Dixie) bridge *{Note: this bridge was at the time a draw-bridge, locally known as Damon's bridge}* – heading north across this bridge, the road ran narrow and straight all the way past County Line Road and into Camp Murphy (Now the State Park). Camp Murphy was already abandoned at that point, but it was a great place to explore and mess around in.

The new wider and higher bridge and highway wiped out a number of businesses and changed the whole character of the area. Before the new bridge was built, just north of the bridge there was plenty of room for numerous businesses along both sides of the road. During the fifties, on the east side of the road right at the north end of the bridge, Ralph's Bar and Grill hung out on pilings over the water. It was so low that on high spring tides and a good wind the waves splashed up through the floor boards. And, they had the biggest and best hamburgers in town. After it was torn down, the old Jupiter Marina on the south side of the bridge took that honor *{Note: The Jupiter Marina is now gone too! It is also interesting to note that diagonally across the street from the Marina – between the road and the railroad tracks – was Damon's (the bridge tender) house – it was also built up on pilings }*.

But back to the north of the bridge; on the southwest corner of Riverside Drive and (then) Old Dixie was Stall's Standard Station and their house; Ted Ledford the milkman worked there also. To the south of that gas station (but still north of the bridge) a new place was built that became Mrs. Murphy's Donut Shop, a new hangout for some of us kids. *{ Note: I still remember that is where a group of us were hanging out when we heard the news that President Kennedy had been shot (1963). It was also the place we read an ad about going to New York, which I'll tell you about later}*. We often parked our boats on shore where the old Ralph's was and walked across the street to Mrs. Murphy's; now it's gone too.

Just to the north of Riverside Drive, but still east of the railroad tracks, (and west of Old Dixie) there were a number of small businesses. My father's construction business, Gladwin-Bassett, Inc. was there; as well as my aunts, Gladwin's Flower Shop; and my uncles, Gladwin's Nursery and Garden Center. My aunt and uncle's places were pretty neat because they had the Flower Shop and the Garden Center tied together with a true old fashion glass green house that was always full of flowering plants and orchids. And, again with no Air Conditioning, it was nice and cool in there. My Grandfather, who everybody called "Pops" worked in that Garden Center for many, many years.

Yes! All of that and more was lost with the continued onslaught of growth. But, I must say that that old bridge was way too narrow to handle two semis trying to cross it at the same time. More than one person fishing the incoming tide (i.e., fishing on the west – no sidewalk – side) had to jump over the rail to avoid being squashed by an oncoming tractor trailer. And, at least one man that I know about, wasn't quick enough and was in fact killed.

XXVIII
CENTENNIAL, DIVE CLUB, CUBA

One of the bigger events to happen in Jupiter when I was younger, was our Centennial Celebration in 1959. It was huge! The area on the south side of the U.S. #1 bridge, east to about where Yarborough Street is (except for Bardens Boating Center, the only boating center around) was vacant and that is where it was held (remember, U.S.#1 and A1A were one and the same road then!)

They had a full size fair set up with all kinds of tents, rides, and displays. Every man in town was 'required' to grow a beard. Even Perry Como, who had just come to town, started growing one. *{Note: He didn't live in the Beach Colony then, he was having a big house built in Tequesta, right across the river from our house on Pennock Point.}* All the women dressed in period clothing. And, I got to demonstrate 'tank diving' in a big plexiglas tank. That was a big thing since 'tank diving' was just coming into its own at the time. The Navy Seals from World War Two and Korea brought it into popularity, and it took a good ten years or more to catch on. One of those Seals, a man named Gunter Muelengracht started up a 'Dive Club' for us kids. I think you had to be fourteen to join. He taught us a great deal about 'safe' diving. One of the cool things he did, was take us to Key West several times. He took us right into the Navel Base, and they took us out on an old landing craft to an island right off the base, and we would stay and dive for a few days. We would eat so many lobsters, we'd get sick of them! I also remember a group of us driving down to the keys during the Cuban Missile Crisis. The entire roadside from one end of the keys to the other was lined with every kind of military vehicle and weapon imaginable. I had never seen anything like it. Massive tractor trailers with every type of missile that we had at the time were set to launch at Cuba. It really wasn't until the crisis was over that we even realized there had been a crisis.

XXIX
THEATERS AND THE HUT

It's funny some of the things that come back to you when you start putting stuff on paper. "Rainbow Bridge" reminded me of where we usually headed when we crossed that bridge – the Drive-in Theater. The Drive-in was always one of the most popular places to go when we were little. Whole families would make a night of it. It was still a very popular place to go on a date when I was in High School in the early sixties. You could also 'splurge' and go to one of the theaters in downtown West Palm Beach, sneaking up to the balcony seating at the Palms Theater with your date was always cool! And then, after the movie, maybe stop at the "Hut" afterwards. The "Hut" was a very popular place for many, many years. In the sixties (while going to Junior College), I worked part time at the Royal Poinciana Playhouse as a valet. During the play, we had time to head over to the Hut and get something to eat. At the playhouse, there was always one old gentlemen that drove his own Rolls Royce (most Rolls Royce's were chauffeur driven) to Opening Night, and we, of course, always tried to be the one to park it. This 'gentleman' was also always one of the last to leave, often staying in the bar until the wee hours of the morning. We were stuck waiting until the last 'valet parking' client left. One night, on a dare, I drove this guy's Roll's with a few of my friends that also were valets, over to the Hut. Boy, did we get noticed. All the 'regulars' at the Hut knew it wasn't mine, but we lucked out when a whole car full of girls (that didn't know us) pulled up right next to 'our' Rolls. That was a fun night! And, yes, I did get the car back with no dents or scratches – maybe a few crumbs; and, we did not get caught!

DOWNRIVER
(Pencil sketch)
<u>*DAG*</u>

THE PELICAN

IF YOU'VE EVER SEEN A PELICAN
THEN SURELY YOU MUST KNOW.
HE'S BIG AND FAT AND UGLY
AND HE'S CERTAINLY QUITE SLOW.

IF YOU'VE EVER WATCHED HIM CATCH A FISH...
...THAT " FREE FALL" CALLED A DIVE.
THEN SURELY YOU MUST WONDER
HOW HE CAN STAY ALIVE.

REMINDS ME OF A KAMIKAZE
DIVE BOMBING ON A BOAT.
THE ONLY THING THAT I CAN SAY,
"IT'S A GOOD THING HE CAN FLOAT!"

BUT WHEN YOU WATCH HIM GLIDING
ACROSS THE OPEN SEA,
THEN YOU'LL KNOW AS I DO,
HE'S AS GRACEFUL AS CAN BE.

THE PELICAN'S A LOT LIKE ME
AND SOMEWHAT LIKE THE BUMBLE BEE.
WE ALL SHOULD KNOW THAT WE CAN'T FLY
BUT I'M THE FIRST TO ASK THEM "WHY?"

FOR I WILL ALWAYS KNOW I CAN,
FOR I HAVE SEEN THE "PELICAN."

DAG

XXX

NEW YORK, NEW YORK

I have to tell another story – it's a long story, but I think it's worth telling. It doesn't really have to do with living in Jupiter, but it does have to do with the kind of things you might do during that period that you would probably never do, or have a chance to do, now. Everybody would be too afraid of lawsuits or whatever.

It was in the early sixties that we got our chance to sail a boat to New York and go to the World's Fair that was being held at that time in Flushing Bay, New York. I'll never forget it! Myself and three friends were sitting in Mrs. Murphy's Donut Shop one Saturday (the old one on the north side of the Alt. A1A bridge). Nothing to do, one of us is reading the "Want Ads" and sees this ad for 'crew members' to sail this sixty-five foot sailboat to New York. Sounded good to us! And, the 'try outs' were that afternoon, so off we go down to the Sailfish Marina on Singer Island. There must have been a hundred or more young guys just like us trying to be one of the six selected. As it happened, all four of us made it – now all we had to do was tell our parents that we were headed for New York on a boat we knew nothing about with an owner whose name we couldn't even remember.

We weren't supposed to leave for a few days, so we thought we had some time. I remember thinking the boat needed some serious work and that maybe I could bring some tools down for a few repairs before we pulled out. When we came down the next morning for our 'orientation' meeting, we were informed that they had decided to leave that same day. We had to run home, pack some clothes and be back by three o'clock. Needless to say, I not only didn't get any repairs done, I didn't even have a chance to bring any tools – and boy did I come to regret that! I do remember that my parents weren't home when I got there to pack, and I ended up leaving them a note that I had already left for New York. Keep in mind that there were no cell phones back then, so our only communication in an emergency was by Ship-to-shore radio with the Coast Guard, or possibly another ship if they were nearby. This means you are quite isolated out there, and that just made this trip all the more interesting. My poor Mom, I don't know how she lived through my 'growing up'.

Anyway, we pulled out of Palm Beach Inlet about six o'clock that night for what should have been a five or six day sail to New York; it ended up taking seventeen days to get there. What a trip, I knew more about sailing than anyone on that boat – and I didn't know a damn thing! We had needed a part for our generator before we left, and the boat owner had it ordered for delivery to Jacksonville for us to pick it up there.

Some place off Cape Kennedy (it was called Cape Canaveral then), we managed to run into our own "Perfect Storm" and was it ever a doozy. The waves built up on those shoals just like the nightmare movies you've seen. They were huge, easily reaching thirty feet or more, and they tossed us around like a bottle cork. One of our halyard lines to a forward jib jammed in the lower block so that we couldn't lower that sail. The wooden block (pulley) was whipping back and forth so hard, the sail was beginning to rip and; of course, there was more sail out than we wanted in a storm like that. One of my friends decided to grab it as it swing across the deck somehow thinking he could hold an entire sail. He was immediately snatched off the boat and was 'sailing' out over the water hanging on the that 'block' for dear life. And, it was his 'life' because if he had let go or fallen off; we could never have gotten the boat turned around to find and pick him up. We managed to bring the boat into the wind enough to swing him back over the boat where we could grab his legs and get him back on board. Finally we got a line on the jammed pulley and haul it down under control. We managed to ride out the rest of the storm without incident.

Trying to find Jacksonville; we came in Saint Augustine Inlet by mistake. Yeah! A big difference, especially considering that this boat we were on drew nine and a half feet of water. Yes, we did run aground before we even got to a dock! We finally managed to work our way right up next to that dock with the fancy restaurant out on the end it (the one that's been there forever, if you've ever been to Saint

Augustine). It was a great place to dock! And, we had a great dinner there! But, I'm not too sure they appreciated having a sixty-five foot sailboat with a bunch of rowdy young guys coming by for a visit.

Anyway, the next morning, we topped off our diesel fuel tank and headed-out for Jacksonville. We learned, "the hard way," that there were no 'inland' charts on this boat; only some old 'open ocean' charts. When we did get into Jacksonville Inlet, we had no idea which way to go. It looked big and wide to the north, so we headed that way. After the "Saint Augustine" incident we weren't about to chance running aground again. We did find it interesting that the whole area was loaded with huge ships – like destroyers and aircraft carriers. But it wasn't until we heard a very loud voice over a giant PA system saying, "WHAT THE HELL'S A SAILBOAT DOING IN HERE?" that we realized we had sailed into the middle of Mayport Naval Station. Within moments a highly armed "Escort" vessel with at least a dozen armed soldiers was showing us the way out. We finally got to the right place, got our part and headed back out to sea.

We ran into bad weather almost immediately after leaving Jacksonville. The constant bobbing up and over big waves caused almost everyone on board to get seasick. I found I was fine as long as I stayed on deck. The smell down below was more than I could handle. I stayed up in the cockpit for several days having someone pass me a peanut butter and jelly sandwich every now and then to 'survive' until the weather (and the smell) cleared. At this point, I had been up for more hours than I can fathom, so I decided to trade out some of my 'watches' for a long needed sleep. As I said earlier, I knew more about boating than anyone else on board, and, as I said – I didn't know anything! But I did know one had to keep figuring out where you thought you were, and where you wanted to be! For that, you needed to keep some kind of course. Well, while I was sleeping, the guy at the helm decided he knew how to sail. He had learned by sailing a dingy around on Long Island Sound. He felt the best way to sail was to just keep the sails full and 'to hell with a course,' and that is the 'course' he passed on to the following 'watches'. When I woke up, two of us used our directional radio antenna to try and determine our approximate location; we realized we were headed on a course that would take us to Bermuda, not New York. As we headed back to the west, we found ourselves "in irons" as they say; no wind, not a breath. We were adrift in a flat calm sea with nothing but rafts of sargrassum seaweed to keep us company. It was then that we found out that the 'fuel' we had picked up in Saint Augustine had been mostly water. It fouled our little diesel and with no tools other than a hatchet, pliers, large screw driver, and a very large pipe wench; we didn't have much to work with. We spent days out there just drifting along in the current of the Gulf Stream. When a little breeze finally did pick up, we started heading for a port hoping to fix our engine.

We were heading into Beaufort Inlet under sail. At least, I think it was Beaufort – that was a long time ago! This boat was difficult enough to handle with an engine, it had an 'offset' screw which meant at low speed you couldn't get any water thrust across the rudder to maneuver. It was also almost impossible to do anything with it at slow speed under sail. So here we are just passing the jetty on an incoming tide, trying to raise the Coast Guard on our radio to get some help to a dock. I will never forget being on the radio with this Coast Guard guy, and he is trying to figure out exactly where we are – and we don't really know! I am standing in the hatchway talking on the radio with him; we are each screaming at each other when I look up and realize that I am seeing a man in a second story window of a Coast Guard building. I can just make out his gestures as he's talking into a mike. He's "my guy." I scream at him to look out his 'G.D. Window', and he sees me. The look on his face was truly unforgettable! He scrambled up some men in a tender, and they managed to get us to a dock before we "got there on our own!" With some clean fuel and a case of 'ether cans' (that's starter fuel), we were on our way again, only this time we decided to stay inland for a while.

The Intracoastal Waterway is really not the place for a boat that draws nine and a half feet of water since they only are required to keep it dredged to a depth of eight and a half feet! We were hardly out of Beaufort when we came to a split channel and didn't know which way to go – remember, no charts? At this point our 'theme song' had become the "Mickey Mouse tune." Remember that? "M, I, C – K, E, Y; M, O, U, S, E." "Mickey Mouse, Mickey Mouse, forever let us hold our banner high!" Yes, we would actually stand on deck and sing that song – right in front of the boat's owner, who of course, was therefore the "Captain" even though he was about eighty-six years old and knew even less than I did – and I already told you about me! Well, we yelled to a small boater as to how to get to the main channel. He told us to follow him, and he then proceeded a few hundred yards back down the way we had come and then cut over to the other channel. Since it took us as long to stop and turn as it did for that guy in the little powder boat to go back down one channel and come back up almost parallel to us in the other channel, our dear ''Captain' didn't pay any attention to the guy's maneuver and proceeded to cut straight across to where to guy was then. Needless to say, we ran high and dry aground – again! And there we stood, singing our song to all the people, and there were quite a few, who had gathered on shore to watch the spectacle. With a lot of help from a lot of laughing boat owners, we finally got off the bar that separated the two channels and back on our way to "New York, New York!"

As I remember, we stayed inland until somewhere around Virginia before heading back out into the open ocean again. That was probably a smart move on our part in as much as we may have never made it going around Cape Hatteras. When we did finally get to the New York harbor some seventeen days after we had left West Palm Beach, it was just at dusk as we passed the Lightship off shore. With no charts, we used what amounted to an old 'road map' to determine that Flushing Bay was somewhere up the East River. Now all we had to do was find the "East River." Again, with our finely tuned navigation expertise, we determined that if we headed straight for the Statue of Liberty, swung just to its north, and then made a hard turn on a particular compass heading, keeping the statue to our stern, we 'SHOULD' hit the East River. Of course, we had no idea if there was any water depth or channel where we were going but did it anyway – and, lucked out! It was dark by this time, and all we could see were thousands and thousands of lights that appeared to be a solid wall. Some places were deep wharfs that we thought might be the river; we kept going, and suddenly realized that we were, if fact, going up 'something,' we just didn't know 'what'! We could tell by the strong current that we must be in the East River, as we kept going the first thing we encountered were the bridges. With almost ninety feet of mast above us, it was impossible to tell if we had clearance under them. We found ourselves in a real predicament. We approached each bridge in as close to a full stop as we could, ready to throw the engine into reverse if we heard or felt the mask hit. Those bridges probable had hundreds of feet of clearance, but there was just no way we could tell. After finding ourselves running up on some rocks (Yes! Again!), we decided to try and anchor up till morning. This was the first time we ever tried to use the dingy we had on deck. *{ Note: We had also had a huge inflatable life raft on board when we left West Palm Beach. But, that was dumped in a trash can in Saint Augustine because we tried to use it there and found out "that's what it was" – "TRASH."}* We lowered the dingy into the water and the first person to step into it had their foot go right through the bottom. Yeah, back to our song!

The next morning, after a few more bumps on the bottom and scrapes with the rocks, we finally reached the Flushing Bay docks. I can't say that they were too happy to see a bunch of ragtag kids and an old man on a beat up old boat trying to maneuver in between the likes of the U.S.S. Constitution and a replica of the Bounty made for the movie, and a few other such fine specimens of ships. Somehow, our boat just didn't fit in, and we were told we had to leave. We found a spot to moor out off of a place called City Island. A small launch was used to ferry people back and forth from their boats. I had my first and only experience with the New York subway system when we traveled back to see the World's Fair. I'm afraid I wasn't impressed by either one! Two days later and nineteen days after we had left, we rented a big station wagon and headed back to dear 'ole Jupiter.

{An interesting "aside" note on that boat! When I got back home and was talking to my Dad about my trip, he reminded me that I had encountered that boat before. It had been the cause of my first "night dive" – a scary thing when you have never done it before and your only source of light is an old W.W.II Navy Seals light (those guys didn't have much in the way of light). Anyway, we were at West End in the Bahamas one night – just inside the marina cut, and we see a light in the eastern sky [the cut runs in from the north] headed right toward us. As we watch, we realize that what we are

seeing is the light of a very big sailboat – yeah!, the same sailboat. This light keeps getting closer and closer – and, there is three hundred plus feet of island between us and them. Suddenly that light stops dead, shaking like a car antenna that's just hit a tree branch. Yeah! Just like when we were on it, it was hard aground – so close to shore that one of the crew jumped off the bow and never even got wet feet. He asked if we could help them get back off the beach. To help them out, we took our boat out and around to their boat, but we could not pull them off – they were just too hard aground. We ended up taking one of their anchors and line out into deep water – putting on our dive equipment and using our wonderful underwater light – we set their anchor hard behind a large coral head. They still had to wait for a higher tide to finally pull themselves free. You'd have thought I'd remembered that before I even signed on to go to New York! But then, I wouldn't have this great story to tell!}

OLD DOG, YOUNG DOG

OLD DOG BRINGS A GRAYING MUZZLE
TO BE RUBBED BETWEEN WARM HANDS.
YOUNG DOG BRINGS BIG WET
PUPPY BREATH KISSES.

OLD DOG BRINGS A TEAR TO MY EYE
AS I WATCH HIM STRUGGLE TO GET UP
AND HEAD DOWN THE HALL,
HIS FAVORITE PLACE TO LIE.

YOUNG DOG BRINGS ME A BALL, WE PLAY…
THEN HE TOO HEADS DOWN THE HALL,
TO CURL TIGHT,
TOUCHING OLD DOG.

OLD DOG, "WHAT'S YOUNG DOG
GOING TO DO WITHOUT YOU?"
"ME TOO?"

DAG

XXXI
PAL, PRINCE & PAUPER, BLAZE, DAWG

I couldn't write about growing up without talking about my dogs. Thinking about each of them was the one thing that hit me the hardest in "going back." Dogs didn't live too long in this area due to the prevalence of Heart Worms *{Note; Heart Warm larvae are transmitted by mosquitoes}*. There was no preventive treatment until fairly recently, so most dogs did not live much beyond five to seven years at the most.

Our first dog at Dubois Park was Pal. He was mostly my dad's dog, but he sure looked after us kids too. He was a beautiful dog, half German Shepherd and half Bloodhound. A big dog, built like a German Shepherd but with the soft short reddish hair and ears of the Bloodhound; but the ears were only about the size of a Weimaraner's ears. A beautiful sweetheart of a dog who loved to hunt for raccoons with my Dad and who could climb a tree as well as any dog I've ever known. And who could forget those soft sad beautiful brown eyes. Jeez! Sounds like I'm talking about a girl I dated.

Next there was Prince and then Pauper , the first time we had two dogs at one time. Pauper, a big Redbone Hound died from a snake bit. He was also the dog who almost died investigating a big 'ol alligator that came to the house one night. But, in Pauper's defense (since some might deem the alligator the smart one and the dog "not so bright.") When an alligator is laying on the beach with his mouth wide open, he doesn't move a muscle. I'm not even sure he breaths, he may just hold his breath as if he were under water. So, to the poor dog, it (the gator) is nothing more than a big hollow log that has washed up on "his" beach – and, there is something inside that log. Lets face it, every other time the dog has come across a hollow log and heard noises coming from inside, he has been in for a fun time. Usually a rabbit, raccoon, or possum came bounding out, and it was, "off to the races."

Gators may not have a very big brain, but two things they know how to do very well. One is how to hunt and the other is how to take care of their young. Trust me, I know about that part (taking care of their young) too! But again, that is another story I may try and get back to!

{Aw, what the heck! This is probably as good a time as any to tell another 'Stupid Boy Story'. What is it about us boys anyway? If you could raise a boy all by his lonesome on a deserted island somewhere, he would probably still get in some trouble. But, not anywhere near as much as if you put him with another boy that's even close to his same age (well, on second thought – the near same age could often mean an age spread as big as 'father and son' or sometimes even 'grandfather and grandson') and you will get somebody daring somebody to do 'something'. Or, if they're not 'daring', they are showing off – either way, it's trouble.

Now, back to my 'Stupid Boy Story,' we – I won't say who 'we' is to protect the other 'we'. Anyway, we were way up the river near Trapper's and we come across some newly hatched alligators – these guys aren't more than a few hours old and boy are they cute. We had a cast net with us, so yes, on a dare one of us throws the cast net over a few of these little guys. Ok yes, it was me! Well you cannot imagine how much noise baby alligators can make and when momma gator heard her babies crying, she came 'a runnin', well, 'a chargin' would be more like it. Remember, we are not in one of today's big strong 'high sided' fiberglass boats – no, we are in a little ten foot long, three foot wide boat made out of one quarter inch thick plywood. And with two of us and all our gear, our freeboard is hardly more than the height of that momma gators' head.

Yes! You're damn right we're scared. Momma gator's banging into the side of the boat; we're trying to use our pole to keep her away, the babies are crying and caught up in the net – yes, we were close to throwing everything overboard just to save our 'you know whats'. We finally managed to get the last baby free of the net and tossed back in the water and no, I have never ever tried to catch a baby alligator again.} Now back to sad dogs stories.

Prince was a perfect compliment to Pauper, he was a small mostly black "Hines 57" variety of dog who thought he was royalty. Prince just had that air about him that he was somehow just a little better than the rest of the dogs in the world. When he was not more than a year or so old, he was bitten on the ear by a snake. He survived and at that point determined that his life's work was to spend the rest of it hunting and killing every snake he came upon both poisonous and nonpoisonous. You could often hear a low muffled barking sound coming from the woods. When you went to investigate, you would find Prince digging deep down into a gopher hole – he wasn't after the gopher; he was after the snake that was down there. How he managed to dig ten feet down a hole and come back out with the snake and not be bitten (again), I will never know.

Bandit, a silver and black little dog about the size of a sheep dog with what looked like a black eye patch over his left eye, was the first dog that seemed almost exclusively "My Dog." He and I spent a lot of time together in the woods. He died from a snake bite also – that was a sad day! I happened to be there when he made it back to the house, his head and neck already so swollen he was having a hard time breathing. At this point in time there were a few "Family Pet" veterinarians available. The nearest one to us being North Palm Beach. I remember loading poor Bandit into the back of my MG and racing for North Palm. We didn't make it!

What is also amazing is that it appeared that both Pauper and Bandit died from the bite of the same snake, but some three or four years apart. We knew that only from the huge size of the bites and the fact that the snake had double fangs – yes, two fangs on each side of his mouth –something apparently quite rare in snakes. For a long time I became like Prince, dedicating my life (or at least, my free time) to hunting for that snake – I never found it!

The last dog of my childhood was "Dawg," half purebred Golden Retriever and half purebred German Shepherd. Yeah! The folks who were raising these "purebred" dogs were not happy when one dog jumped the fence – I on the other hand, thought the "mix" made a great new bred. I brought Dawg home when I was just out of high school, so he ended up being my little sisters dog more than mine. But those dogs, each and everyone of them, were the best friend(s) I ever had! And, yes – I still have "Mutts" at home.

Another interesting side note about having dogs back in the fifties and sixties (and maybe beyond) is the fact that no one had fenced in yards at the time. Everyone's dogs were free to run the neighborhood and, they often did! This was most often during the day while we kids were in school and/or their owners were off at work. But, what was interesting is that they all seemed to work out their own hierarchy and therefore you rarely saw any dog fights. Each dog did know where his own property was, and he would usually only get defensive about other dogs intruding his personal space. And, our dogs, like everyone else's dogs always knew what time the school bus brought us home and they would be laying at the end of our driveways – waiting.

HAVE YOU EVER WONDERED?

HAVE YOU EVER PICKED A FLOWER
JUST TO SMELL ITS SWEET BOUQUET,
KNOWING WHEN YOU PICKED IT,
IT WOULD LAST BUT JUST A DAY?

HAVE YOU EVER WATCHED A BUTTERFLY
AS ITS BEAUTY DID UNFOLD?
IT MADE YOU WANT TO KEEP IT
JUST FOR YOU TO HAVE AND HOLD.

TO WATCH IT FLUTTER IN THE AIR
AND FROLIC ALL ABOUT,
BUT KNOWING IN A DAY OR TWO
ITS LIFE WOULD SOON BURN OUT!

HAVE YOU EVER FOUND A SEASHELL
JUST LYING ON THE SAND?
YOU PICK IT UP SO GENTLY
AND PLACE IT IN YOUR HAND.

IT SPARKLED IN THE SUNLIGHT
THIS BEAUTY FROM THE SEA
AND YOU PLACE IT IN A SPECIAL PLACE
FOR ALL THE WORLD TO SEE.

NOW THINK ABOUT THE LIFE OF EACH---
THE FLOWER, FLY, AND SHELL---
IS ONE'S LIFE REALLY BETTER,
OR CAN WE EVER TELL?

(Continued on next page)

HAVE YOU EVER WONDERED?
(Continued from previous page)

THE SHELL SPENDS LIFE IN DARK AND GLUM
AT THE BOTTOM OF THE SEA,
ONLY WHEN IT YIELDS TO DEATH
ITS BEAUTY DO WE SEE.

NOW BUTTERFLIES AND FLOWERS,
THEY SPEND THEIR LIFE IN SPLENDOR;
BUT WHEN THEY TOO SUCCUMB TO DEATH,
THERE IS NOTHING TO REMEMBER.

HAVE YOU EVER WONDERED,
WHICH ONE YOU'D LIKE TO BE –
A FLOWER, OR A BUTTERFLY
OR A SHELL BENEATH THE SEA?

THINK ABOUT THE LIFE OF EACH...
WHAT WISDOM IT MIGHT TEACH...
IS THERE ONE YOU'D LIKE TO BE?
OR,...A LITTLE OF ALL THREE?

DAG

XXXII
SANDSPURS AND GOATHEADS

No story of growing up in Jupiter (or anywhere in South Florida for that matter) would be complete without discussing (or maybe 'just cussing') the sandspur. And, if you are on the coast, then the goathead must also be included. Sandspurs love sandy disturbed soil – and boy did we have a lot of sandy 'disturbed' soils what with the phenomenal growth we were experiencing.

As a true connoisseur of the Sandspur or, more properly – sandbur, the first thing to know is that we have at least two very distinct varieties. One, the more common one today, is a low growing grass that can spread by both its burs (your dog is a great 'spreader' of sandburs) and by sending out runners just like a Saint Augustine type grass – only not quite that prolific. This is most common today for just one reason – lawn mowers. Because it's low growing, lawn mowers don't always get the bur spikes cut off before they mature ; and even if they do, it can still spread as a 'runner'. The second type, which is the one I really want to talk about is a 'single clump' plant something like a Bermuda type grass only much bigger and better than that! These sandburs (alright, proper or not, I've got to call them what we always called them, "sandspurs") were huge and healthy (often reaching heights of 18" or more), they were our nemesis. They constantly gave us flat tires on our bikes and riding home on a flat tire is just no fun.

Now Goatheads were (and still are) worse for this (flat tires) but for the most part Goatheads were only a problem over by the beach. The only reason I brought goatheads into this discussion was because, one, they are a beautiful creation of the devil. You really owe it to yourself to look at a Goathead up-close and personal. They do look just like a goats head with two big horns (Spikes) positioned perfectly so that no mater how the head (the bur) falls, one thorn (horn) is always sticking straight up – and it <u>will</u> draw blood. The second reason for bringing up the Goathead is the masterful deception of the plant that produces it. The plant is beautiful, low rich green leaves that look deceptively like soft ferns and the prettiest yellow flowers spread amongst this beautiful green backdrop. If you are a tourist, you just can't stop yourself from stepping right in there and picking one of those beautiful flowers – and boy will you wish you hadn't! And, even if you weren't after the flower, that plant just looks so inviting as a way to get those tender yankee feet off that hot sand or pavement. Again, you have to remember the time period – there were few, if any, paved parking areas at the beaches – you just pulled off the road. Also, there were no 'dune walk-overs' or any such thing as "flip-flops" or the like.

But, I've got to get back to those sandspurs. They <u>were</u> everywhere, as more and more land was cleared there were more and more sandspurs. Of course, the sides of the roads were some of the worst since they were rarely (if ever) mowed. Because of that, these sandspurs got huge; and, as boys, that just made them enticing – somehow we just couldn't help ourselves. When a group of us was walking down a road, a few of us would just have to linger back behind the others and pick some of these big beautiful green stalks of sandspurs (the dried stalks were no good – they didn't have any weight!) Then, just at the right moment we would flip these things right into the small of the backs of the guys in front of us – then, we'd run like hell. These stalks were big, and they were heavy (think of a lollypop with a much longer handle) and you could really 'flip' them out there with a lot of force. Now once this mass of spikes has gone through your T-shirt and into your back you are in a real predicament because as soon as you try to reach back there and pull the damn thing out, your T–shirt tries to pull tight dragging this mass of burs sideways and making things even worse. Yup! That was a lot of fun – As long as 'you' were one of the guys in back! But even then, it usually resulted in one big sandspur throwing fight.

I also have to describe the way we 'got to the other side' of a field or empty (building) lot that was full of sandspurs. In this case, it wasn't the green burs on the plant that were a problem; it was the thousands and thousands of dried burs that scattered everywhere around the plant. It is true that most of us had feet as tough as nails, but our feet had their "achilles heel" – it just wasn't our heel. It (they) were that tender little area between our toes and the balls of our feet, and also the area on each side of our arch – neither of which ever had a chance to get toughened up. And so, we learned this special walk – actually, more like a dance – to get us across these fields.

It is a very special dance with very special moves requiring some degree of advanced planing. The first thing you do is study the vacant lot to determine the best possible 'path' to take. What you are looking for is the path with the most open sandy areas, i.e. fewest sandspur plants and, that are close enough together to step from one open area to the next. You had to use a lot of forethought here, because the best looking path may just 'dead end' after you are halfway across – and, in some cases that could be a very long way. Once you had committed to 'your' path, you started 'your dance'. Keep in mind that these seemingly opened areas weren't really 'opened,' they just appeared that way. Actually, they were covered in dry burs and that is where the 'dance' came into play.

The dance went something like this – from position number one, (which is wherever you are standing at that moment) you looked for the best possible place to set your foot into 'open area' number two. There is NEVER an area big enough to just step onto it without getting sandspurs. The secret was in the step, you had to point your toes straight down and then just look for a place just big enough for your toes. If you couldn't even find an area that big, one went to step number three which was curling your toes as tightly as possible and, using just your toenails, scrap enough burs forward to give you that little space. This often resulted in at least a few burs getting into the quick on the sides of your nails, again, resulting in step number four – balancing on one foot in the middle of a sandspur patch while you pulled the burs out of the other foot. Once this is successfully accomplished you can then go back to step number one. Pointing your toes as straight down as you possibly can, you gingerly press them into that little open area you created. This is very soft pure white Florida sugar sand we are talking about, so your toes will go in some distance before there is any real resistance. It is at that point that you allow yourself to bear weight and stand on you 'tippy-toes'. And, 'tippy' toes they are, with the soft sand there is no real support to help keep your balance – and this is where your dance can end! As you progress across this field of burs, balancing, clearing, and stepping from one tippy-toe to the next; disaster is always close at hand. It is one thing to balance on one foot, it is another to balance tip-toe on one foot. And, it is yet another all together different thing to do all this while trying to use the other foot to reach several feet away and gently scrape burs off the surface of that sand – again, with just your toenails – and, you must be ambidextrous (feet wise) since you will be doing this dance on alternating steps. If, God forbid, you 'screw up' and lose your balance – YOU WILL REGRET IT. One of two things will happen, either you will take several fast little steps in the direction of your fall – trying to regain your balance – in which case BOTH feet will be covered in sandspurs. OR, even more horrendous, you truly lose your balance completely and FALL OVER – resulting in real pain – sandspurs in your hands, your arms, your legs, your body, and yes, sometimes even in your face. The sandspur dance was not a dance for the faint of heart.

And no matter how good you are, the one sandspur that most often hurts the worst is the one you get in the most tender part of your finger while pulling it out of the toughest part of your foot!

THE DOGS YARD
(Pencil sketch)
<u>*DAG*</u>

OLD TREE

THERE IS AN OLD TREE THAT GROWS IN MY YARD,
ITS BRANCHES ALL TWISTED BROKEN AND SCARRED.

ITS TRUNK LIKE A PIECE OF BURNT LEATHER HIDE,
KINKED IN THE MIDDLE SO IT LEANS TO ONE SIDE.

THERE'S SOMETHING SPECIAL ABOUT THAT OLD TREE IN
THE DARK OF NIGHT – IT SPEAKS TO ME.

I HEAR A WHISPER IN ITS LEAVES
THAT I DON'T HEAR IN OTHER TREES.

IT SPEAKS OF LIVING, SPEAKS OF LIFE.
IT SPEAKS OF HARDSHIP, SPEAKS OF STRIFE.

THE OTHER TREES THAT GROW NEARBY,
JUST AS STRAIGHT AND JUST AS HIGH.

THEY DON'T KNOW LIFE – THEY'VE JUST BEGUN.
THEY DON'T KNOW STRIFE – THEY'RE JUST TOO YOUNG

BUT THAT OLD TREE IT SPEAKS TO ME
WHEN LATE AT NIGHT, WHILE OTHERS SLEEP,

BELOW IT I SIT AS THE DOUBTS THEY DO CREEP.
THEN I LOOK UP AND SEE THAT MAJESTIC OLD TREE.

A BLACK SILHOUETTE AGAINST THE NIGHT SKY,
ITS BOUGHS BENT DOWN LOW, LIKE A GESTURING SIGH.

IT SPEAKS OF ITS LIFE IN THE WINDS AND THE RAINS;
OF THE LIMBS THAT IT LOST IN PAST HURRICANES.

IT SPEAKS OF THE LIGHTNING AND THUNDER ENDURED;
AND SOME HOW JUST KNOWING, I AM ASSURED.

DAG

XXXIII

GOOD AND BAD

Yes! There were some great times growing up in Jupiter during that period. 'Listening to,' not 'watching' "Gun Smoke" on the radio on Saturday night as a kid. Laying on the roof counting shooting stars. Shining a light on the river and watching it come alive with thousands of jumping mullet. Catching more fish than you knew what to do with, falling to sleep to the sound of crickets and frogs, and especially, the sound of a million mosquitoes at you window screen. And, literally owning the river all to yourself and going to a beach with absolutely <u>no one</u> on it. I do miss a lot of it. But, then I like Air Conditioning and having a grocery store right down the road. And I'm sure if I were a teenager, I would love not having to use the one and only 'hard wired' phone in the middle of the living room, where all my brothers and sisters and parents could hear every word of my being 'shot down' for a date. Yes, every "time" has its good and bad, but growing up in Jupiter in the fifties and sixties was a whole lot more "good" than "bad."

MUSIC IN THE RAINDROPS

THERE'S A MUSIC IN THE RAINDROPS,
A SADNESS IN THEIR SOUND.
WATCHING AT MY WINDOW'S PANE
EACH TEAR COMES RUNNING DOWN.

EACH SPLASH UPON THE WINDOW'S SILL
CRACKS OPEN SECRET SONGS.
SONGS STORED DEEP IN CATACOMBS
THAT LIE WITHIN MY MIND.

'MEMORIES' – LOCKED AWAY SO LONG
THAT KEYS COULD NOT BE FOUND.
'MEMORIES'– FILED AND STORED SO DEEP –
SO SAFE IT SOMEHOW SEEMED.

TILL RAINDROPS FALLING, SEEPING, FOUND –
THE MUSIC REAPPEARS –
NOSTALGIC MELANCHOLIC SONGS
WISTFUL YEARNING TUNES.

AS TEARS UPON MY WINDOW'S PANE;
AS DROPLETS ON MY SILL –
JUST SECRET SONGS I ONCE HAD SUNG
NOW FIND I KNOW THEM STILL.

RAINDROPS FALLING SOFTLY NOW,
A SADNESS IN THEIR SOUND.
WATCHING AT MY WINDOW'S PANE;
EACH TEAR COMES RUNNING DOWN.

__DAG__

XXXIV
LAST TIMES

When you "go back" and start remembering things from your past, it's interesting what comes up. Ron Wiggins (columnist for the Palm Beach Post) often writes about "Last Times." In writing and remembering things from my past, I couldn't help but think about "Last Times." Do you remember the last time: You heard a screen door slam behind you? The last time you used a stick, your fishing pole, or your hand or leg, to "light up" the phosphorus in the river? The last time you shined (or could shine) a light across the river and watched ten thousand mullet go wild? The last time you went skinny dipping (No! In your pool doesn't count)? The last time you experienced what "dark" really is? By that, I mean being outside somewhere where there is no light of any kind for at least twenty miles – remember what the stars REALLY look like? Remember the last time you broke a window with a ball, or rock, or, for some of us, most anything?

I just have to tell you about the last broken window. Well, it's not really 'my' last broken window; it's really the last one I remember my brother breaking. *{Hey, I don't mind tattling on my brother at this point. He could be pretty mean at times. Heck, ask him about the time he hit me in the eye with a 'needle dart' [Remember those? Kitchen match, needle, and a piece of paper.] He promised to give me everything he had or* *ever would have if I just wouldn't tell our parents – I KEPT MY END OF THE DEAL and HE DIDN'T }* Anyway, we were running a phone line across the roof (on Pennock Point) so that we could have our own phone in our room *{Two things to remember at this time. One, running a second phone line was illegal and two, having an unregistered phone was illegal. Bellsouth had a monopoly on all phones and phone lines at the time.}* I forgot exactly where we had 'procured' the phone, but maybe that's just as well.

So, as it happens I am inside the house when this happens. Skip's laying flat on the roof reaching down and back up under the roof overhang trying to drive in a nail to hold up the wire. Of course, as always, the windows are opened – and as are many of today's windows, these were the 'awning type' windows. The frames were wood, not aluminum like today but otherwise the same – AND, they were wide open, ALL FOUR VENTS of glass – straight out, just waiting for this moment.

You really already know the rest, the hammer drops and hits the first vent – and from there everything was like slow motion. The glass didn't break completely right away, it just cracked. It seemed like it took forever to break through with a tinkle and then a plunk as it hit the second piece of glass. And yes again, more slow motion! Tinkle, plunk! Pause, tinkle, plunk! Then one last pause-tinkle-plunk and the hammer's on the ground. By this time I am rolling on the floor laughing and of course the more I laugh the angrier Skip gets. He runs to the other side of the roof to jump on the TV antenna pole (our usual means of accessing and disembarking our roof) in order to come take his frustrations out on me. Well as he's heading in the back door, I'm heading out the front door (Yes, still laughing. I know that wasn't helping much, but I just couldn't stop). I decide to run into our shed because I know I can brace the door to keep him out. And that's where the finale took place, I've got my thumbs in my ears making faces through the glass door at him and he just can't stand it. He walks over by the fruit trees, picks off the biggest Grapefruit he can find and, HURDLES this thing right through the door. Yup! The grand finale of 'last times' – five windows. Wow!

Yes, I could go on for ever!

{Okay Mom, "I hope I did you proud!"}

IDEAS YET TO WRITE!

- Bee Hives & Honey.
- Little League Baseball 1955 – took all of Jupiter and Hope Sound to make a team
- Rope Swing @ Trappers, and the Cable Ropes (originally put up for Camp Murphy) up river
- No keys – for anything other than the one that stayed on the floorboard of the jeep
- Girls playing Jacks and wearing Skates keys
- Playing with the porpoises that came up river
- Fire fishing and gigging my first big Drum fish
- When Cracker Jacks had "Real Toys"
- Cereal Boxes – Little baking soda Submarine
- Periwinkles & sucking nectar from wild hibiscus
- Jealousy Windows
- Old Radios, TV's, # of channels & Antenna
- Sawgrass on Pennock Point
- Telephones & Party lines
- The 12 foot wide by forty plus feet long computer on the third floor of the Business Administration building at U of F.
- "Watching Submarine Races"- that's what we called it when we parked on the beach with a date. The real "human powered" submarine races (sponsored by FAU and Perry Submarine) in middle 70's ruined it!
- Schools of mullet over a half-mile long and quarter mile wide right on the beach and everything from sailfish to sharks diving in and out of them. These were the same schools that came in the inlet and filled the river from shore to shore.
- Waking in the night to the sound of the ocean pounding – being able to hear it from anywhere in Jupiter.
- Laying on the dock until your chest ached while you stared into the shadows to watch blow fish eating barnacles or oysters making like squirt guns as the tide went out

☐ *PLACES REFERRED TO IN THE BOOK*
(and not named on the maps)
☐ *Are shown to the left (pg. 165)*
Notice the Buildings (Gladwin, etc.) located between the railroad tracks and Old Dixie Highway.

Remember, EVERY road was a narrow two lane road at the time.

See also The two page map on pages 169-170

THE RIVER'S GONE

THE RIVER'S GONE THAT I ONCE KNEW
THE RIVER WHERE A YOUNG LAD GREW –
TO BE THE MAN THAT NOW DOES STAND
UPON HER SHORES TO VIEW...

A CONNEY ISLAND VISTA
AND A RINGLING CIRCUS TOO!
EVERYTHING'S SO STRANGE AND NEW,
THE HOUSES, BOATS, AND, PEOPLE TOO!

OH SURE, THERE'S STILL A FEW LANDMARKS
THE KIND THAT I ONCE KNEW.
THE LIGHTHOUSE, MY HOUSE...
AT LEAST ARE TWO.

BUT STILL, EVERYTHING'S SO NEW –
THE HOUSES TRUE, BUT EVEN THE TREES ARE NEW!
MY SON TOO – UPON THIS RIVER GREW...
JUST NOT THE ONE THAT I ONCE KNEW!

__DAG__

PS: Conney Island is the nick name we've given the big
sandbar in the river
where everyone congregates on the weekends.

Self Portrait
(Pencil sketch)
DAG
(Yeah, a long time ago!)

*Find me on Facebook for more
Old Jupiter Pictures*

To contact the Author:

Dan Gladwin
11041 SE Harken Terrace
Jupiter, FL 33469
MyJupiterBook@gmail.com

*Poems and stories
Reg. Copyright
2006 & 2007*

VISIT THE WEB SITE

MyJupiterBook.com

MyJupiterPhotos.com

Find my books on Amazon.com
"Brenda's Story"
"Songs for the tone Deaf"

See corresponding number *[#]
on Pages 171-172

*[1] Girl Scout Camp, now Bay Harbour
*[2] Twelve acres dad could buy for $1200
*[3] Duck Ponds
*[4] Steel's Creek and location of Stills
*[5] The Wooten's house – where he shot the snook
*[6] Jackson Property – now my house
*[7] Pennock Dairy
*[8] Jupiter School
*[9] Congregational Church
*[10] Southern Methodist Church & Old Town Hall
*[11] Michael's Meat Market

After you finish the book please visit the web site
MyJupiterBook.com
for some related pictures
and additional poems and sketches.

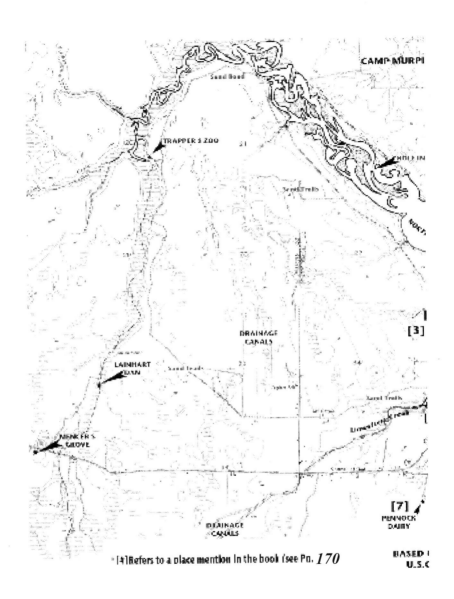

*[*]Refers to a place mention in the book (see Pg. *170*

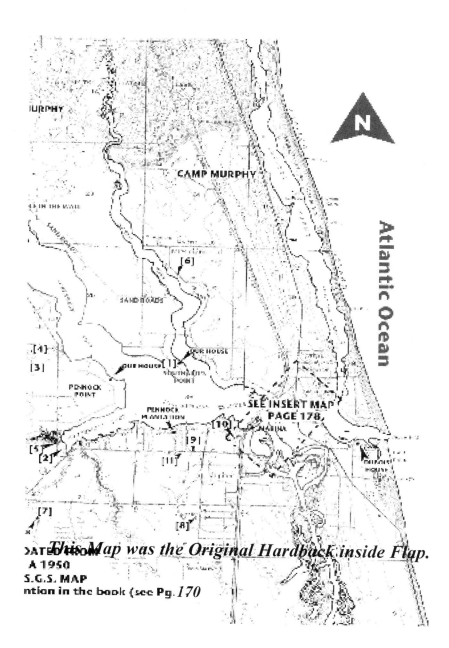